THE
BARBECUE
COOK

The photograph on the front cover shows Spring Kebabs (page 98), Peppered Steak Kebabs (with Mustard Dressing, page 107) and Vegetable Skewers (with Lentil Dhal, page 104). Photograph by David Perks, Chorley and Handford, Wallington, Surrey.

THE
BARBECUE
COOK

Annette Yates

RIGHT WAY

CONTENTS

THE BARBECUE COOK

This barbecue cook has always been an enthusiast of outdoor cooking. It all began during early childhood days when I would cook small potatoes on a roughly-made fire of sticks, by the River Taf, at Ponsticill on the edge of the Brecon Beacons. The potatoes were always black and shrivelled, but to my friends and to me they were simply delicious.

The next step was to Girl Guide camps on the Gower coast, where my turfing and fire-building skills were tested, together with my ability to cook breakfast for what seemed like hundreds of hungry mouths.

From there I progressed to camping holidays, firstly as a student and then with my husband and small daughters. As a family we have had some wonderful outdoor culinary experiences, the most memorable having been in Scotland and in France. It was in Biscarosse in Aquitaine that we first grilled fresh sardines and langoustines on the barbecue – delicious with a green salad and a freshly-baked baguette.

Since then barbecuing has always held a fascination for me. After all, what better way of relaxing and gathering your family and friends together. 'Having a barbecue' is such a leisurely, healthy and fun way of cooking and eating – and the fresh air always seems to stimulate appetites so that everyone eats more heartily than usual.

More recently I have discovered the joys of a gas barbecue – nothing extravagent – a portable, fold-away model. With it, barbecuing can be an almost daily occurrence in summer. It has been a wonderful assistant during the writing of this book, both in the development of new recipes and in the updating of old favourites. I hope that 'The Barbecue Cook' will be an inspiration to both first-time and experienced barbecue cooks everywhere.
Enjoy yourselves!

Annette Yates

1. THE BARBECUE

To barbecue is to cook (or smoke) foods over an open fire. A modern barbecue consists of a box to contain the fire, over which sits a metal grid to hold the food. There is a wide variety to choose from today. Look in hardware shops, supermarkets, department stores, cookshops, garden centres and DIY stores.

For those of you who are buying your first barbecue, and for those of you who may be updating your current model, I have listed some useful tips together with brief descriptions of the types available.

TIPS FOR CHOOSING A BARBECUE
When you are thinking of buying a barbecue, consider:

- what is available – see the descriptions of barbecue types below.

- where you will use a barbecue. Will you want to move it around? If so, will you need a portable model? Is your garden suitable for a built-in version, and will you use it often enough to warrant building it?

- the quality. Do you want something which is sturdy and will last, or are you buying a barbecue as an experiment – to see if you will enjoy the style of cooking before investing in a more costly version?

- its stability. Check that the barbecue is stable on a level surface – particularly those on a stand, legs or wheels.

- the height of the barbecue – is it comfortable to use?

- storage during the winter. Where you will store it may well affect your choice – look at sizes and whether they can be dismantled.

- the handles. Are they insulated? Is there sufficient room between the handle and the hot surface to avoid burning your hands?

- the size of the cooking area – imagine how many chops, burgers, cobs of corn, etc., it will hold. How many are you likely to be cooking for on a regular basis? How many batches of food would you need to cook in order to serve the guests?

- the cooking grid – the bars should not be so far apart that they allow the food to fall through.

The Disposable Barbecue
This is a small, lightweight, inexpensive barbecue, ideal for cooking small amounts of food on picnics or while camping. It is designed to be thrown away after use. A foil tray with a metal grid contains specially-impregnated coals. It is easy to light, the coals are ready in about 15 minutes, and it lasts about an hour. The foil tray gets extremely hot, so it needs to be put on a suitable surface. Take care on windy days – they can tip over.

The Portable Barbecue
The smallest barbecue is a hibachi (Japanese for fire bowl). A small stand supports a sturdy metal fire bowl which holds the charcoal, and one to four metal grids for

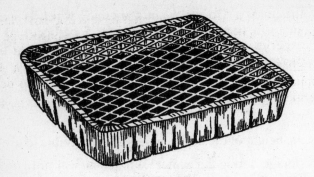

The Disposable Barbecue

the food. The grids usually have wooden handles so the food can be moved, on notches, away from or towards the heat. Air vents in the fire bowl are designed to control the heat of the fuel. A portable barbecue can be used on a table and will cook for two to four people at a time.

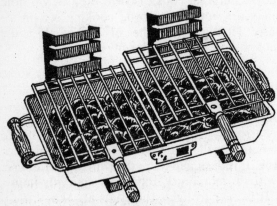

The Portable Barbecue

'Fold-away' versions are available in various sizes, weights and quality. Some fold away into a mini case, and some have a lid or windshield and detachable legs, or legs which also act as a handle for carrying.

The Freestanding Barbecue
This type is available in a variety of shapes, sizes, qualities

and prices. It is usually supported by legs and has a larger cooking area than the portable version. The basic type has a round or rectangular fire bowl on legs, a grid with variable heights, and a windshield. Some include a shelf beneath the fire bowl, a serving shelf on the side, a warming rack, or a rod for spit roasting.

The Freestanding Barbecue

A kettle barbecue is a freestanding model with a lid. The vented lid is used as a windshield to protect the food and fuel if it rains, to control the smoke, and to speed up the cooking of meat joints and whole poultry.

The Wagon Barbecue
This type is generally much larger and more expensive. A large rectangular fire bowl and grid are supported by two legs and two wheels, enabling it to be moved around (wheelbarrow style) with ease. It may have shelves on the sides, space for hanging utensils, shelving underneath the firebox, warming racks above the fire area, and a lid. Some have an additional firebox which can be used in a vertical position for spit roasting, while some have a removable firebox so that the wagon or trolley can be folded and stored flat.

The Wagon Barbecue

The Built-in Barbecue
A permanent barbecue can be an attractive garden or patio fitting and is appealing if you are serious about barbecuing. Simple, self-assembly kits are usually inexpensive but you need to consider the additional cost of bricks – you will need about a hundred. They can be cemented together for a permanent fixture or stacked for dismantling at any time. Follow the assembly instructions carefully. The kit comes with a metal base, a charcoal grid and a large cooking grid. Pegs are usually supplied for embedding in the wall, to give adjustable cooking levels.

The Gas Barbecue
In place of charcoal, a gas barbecue uses liquid petroleum gas (usually butane) to heat lava rock. The hot lava rock then heats the food. The traditional barbecue flavour of the food is just the same – as the fats and juices from the food drip on to the hot coals or rocks they vaporise to give the 'smoke' which, in turn, gives the food its flavour.

A gas barbecue is convenient – easy to light, quick (it is ready for cooking in 10-15 minutes), clean (it does not produce a lot of smoke during the initial lighting up and the lava rock is re-usable) and costs about the same to run

The Built-in Barbecue

The Gas Barbecue

as the charcoal version. The small, portable model has legs which fold into a handle for carrying (the gas bottle is separate). Large, more sophisticated wagon barbecues are available with several burners and adjustable controls. Always follow the manufacturer's instructions for using a gas barbecue, and find yourself a reliable supplier of replacement lava rock.

Rotisseries
Except for disposable and small portable barbecues, most

models will facilitate a battery-operated rotisserie. It is usually purchased separately. Check with the manufacturer's instructions for fitting.

ESSENTIAL BARBECUE ACCESSORIES
A thick, sturdy apron
Good oven gloves
Long-handled tongs
Long-handled fish slice
Long-handled brush for basting foods on the barbecue – with natural bristle, not nylon or plastic which will melt on the hot surface
Long, flat metal skewers
Hinged wire grid – to enclose burgers, fish and small pieces of food, to make turning them easier
Wire brush – for cleaning the barbecue grid

FUEL FOR THE BARBECUE
Most barbecues use charcoal (partly-burnt wood) which is obtainable as lumpwood and as briquettes. Lumpwood is easier to light while briquettes burn for longer. Charcoal substitutes are available – usually labelled 'barbecue fuel' or 'barbecue briquettes'. I tend to avoid these, since they do not burn as well as charcoal. Always store charcoal in a dry place.

Self-igniting charcoal is more expensive than the plain lumpwood and briquettes, but is a useful stand-by if you want to speed up the lighting process, or if you lack the confidence to start a barbecue from scratch.

Lava rock for gas barbecues is more expensive than charcoal but it can be used over and over again. Replace it with new rock when it becomes soiled with fat. You will know when it needs changing because the lava rock will flare up frequently during cooking.

BASIC BARBECUE TIPS
● Plan ahead, preparing as much as possible in advance. Don't try and cook everything on the barbecue.

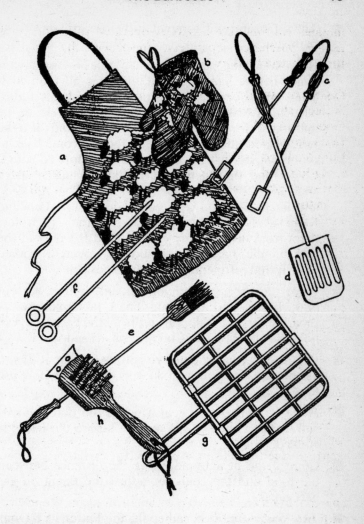

Essential Barbecue Accessories
(a) Apron
(b) Oven gloves
(c) Long-handled tongs
(d) Long-handled fish slice
(e) Long-handled brush
(f) Long, flat metal skewers
(g) Hinged wire grid
(h) Wire brush

- Thaw frozen food completely before grilling on the barbecue.

- Remember the simple hygiene rules – wash your hands before handling food and keep all food cool, clean and covered. Refrigerate all perishable foods, particularly fish and meat. Meat which is to be marinated for more than 2 hours should also be refrigerated (allow refrigerated food to come back to room temperature for about an hour before cooking). Cook food thoroughly, particularly, chicken, pork and sausages. Keep cooked food away from raw food and keep raw food covered outside before cooking. Keep salads and other foods covered too – to protect them from insects. Any cooked food left over at the end of the barbecue should be covered, cooled quickly and refrigerated as soon as possible.

- Have the necessary equipment, oil, butter, season-ings, bastes and the food on a table nearby. A separate serving table, further from the barbecue, can hold the plates, cutlery, breads, salads and so on.

- Oil the barbecue grid before putting food on it. If you use hinged wire grids and skewers, oil them before use too.

- Avoid grilling over a heat which is too fierce. Foods will dry and burn on the outside before the inside is cooked.

- Control the heat by adjusting the distance between the food and the coals, or adjust the flame on gas barbecues.

- The longer the food can cook, the better its flavour will be. Quick-cooking foods have little time to achieve that certain barbecue flavour.

- Flare-ups, caused by too much dripping fat, blacken the food and give it a strong, disagreeable, smoky flavour.

- Add an unusual flavour to barbecued food by

scattering chips of wood such as hickory or mesquite (soaked in water first) over the hot charcoal. For gas barbecues, wrap the soaked wood in pierced foil before placing it on the lava rock.

● Fresh herbs give a lovely aroma when thrown on to the barbecue – use rosemary, thyme and fennel. Try lavender too.

● Look after your barbecue and it will last you a long time. Allow the charcoal to burn out and the barbecue to cool completely before clearing out and disposing of the ashes.

● Clean the barbecue ready for its next use. Use a wire brush to clean the cooking grid, then wash it well in hot soapy water. It is a good idea to rinse it in (or spray it with) an anti-bacterial cleaner. Brush out any remaining coals and ashes from the fire box, and scrape away fat and any stubborn burns. There are several products available for cleaning barbecues.

LIGHTING TIPS

● Barbecues without a separate coal grate can be lined with foil, shiny side towards the coals. The foil will reflect the heat up towards the food, and it will help to keep the barbecue clean too.

● Use barbecue firelighters or special barbecue lighter liquids or gels to start a charcoal fire (please read the safety tips below). Follow the pack instructions for using barbecue lighting aids. Alternatively, use self-igniting charcoal.

● Light a charcoal barbecue 30-40 minutes before you want to cook – the coals will take this time (or longer) to light up and to achieve an even, flame-free heat. A gas barbecue needs only 10-15 minutes.

● Use a taper to light the barbecue, rather than a match.

● The coals are ready when they have turned greyish-white in daylight (or glowing red in the dark) and all the flames have died away. If the coals are glowing red it may still be too hot to cook the food very close to the coals. As a guide, you should be able to hold your hand a few inches away from the coals for 2-3 seconds.

● Charcoal should burn steadily for about an hour and a half. If you need to add extra, place small amounts around the edge of the fire and gradually move it to the centre, with long tongs or a poker, as it ignites. Resist the temptation to add piles of cold charcoal – they will only slow down the fire.

SAFETY TIPS

● Always follow the manufacturer's instructions for lighting, using and cleaning a barbecue.

● Always barbecue outdoors.

● Set the barbecue on a level surface, away from bushes, trees and fences.

● Never light a barbecue with petrol, paraffin or methylated spirits.

● Never move a barbecue once it is lit.

● Never leave a flaming barbecue unattended.

● Don't allow children to play near a lit barbecue.

● Keep a bucket of sand or garden soil handy – in case the barbecue should catch fire. Smothering it with sand or earth is the safest way to put out the flames.

● Use good oven gloves – to protect yourself from hot skewers, dishes and the barbecue itself.

● Use long-handled tongs and fish slices, and brushes for marinades – again to prevent burns.

● Allow portable barbecues time to cool before handling them to take home. Charcoal and wood that looks grey may still be extremely hot, so take care.

BARBECUE BACK-UPS

To get the best from your barbecue it makes sense to use other kitchen equipment to complement it and to help each barbecue occasion to be successful every time.

The refrigerator is probably the most important back-up to the barbecue and, in my opinion, the larger it is, the better. It is vital (particularly in warm weather) for chilling the salads, dressings, sauces and desserts you may have prepared in advance; plus all the vegetables, fish, poultry and meat which you intend to cook on the barbecue. Aways keep foods covered in the fridge and store raw fish, poultry and meat on a shelf lower than the one holding cooked food and salads. For best results, foods which are to be grilled on the barbecue should be allowed to return to room temperature before cooking. Many salads prefer to be served at room temperature too – the flavour is so much better – while many desserts are nicer chilled. So it is worth doing a little planning before the event, perhaps making lists of what to take out of the refrigerator and when.

The freezer is very convenient for storing raw fish, poultry and meat prior to barbecuing. Remember to allow all foods to thaw completely before barbecue cooking. If necessary, make yourself a list of foods to be taken from the freezer and when. If you know that you will be short of time during the days prior to a barbecue, consider what you can prepare well in advance and freeze – sauces, dips, cooked rice or pasta, or the desserts.

Now that over 50% of households have a *microwave* or *a combination cooker*, it is worth mentioning the advantages of using one to back up the barbecue.

Speed up cooking on the barbecue, particularly when you are entertaining large numbers, by cooking some foods in the microwave before grilling them on the barbecue – sausages and chicken pieces, for example. By doing this you will be quite confident that food coming off the barbecue is cooked right through and is unlikely to give your guests a tummy upset.

When you serve rice or pasta as an accompaniment to barbecued food, remember that both of them reheat beautifully in the microwave. So cook them several hours or a day ahead, either conventionally or in the microwave, cover and refrigerate in serving dishes overnight (or freeze them for longer). Then simply reheat them in the microwave just before serving on the day of the barbecue.

Reheat sauces in the microwave – in suitable jugs ready for serving.

Cook potatoes in their jackets, ready for browning and crisping on the barbecue (see page 118).

COOKING FOR LARGE PARTIES

Cooking for a large party needs a little extra planning. Here are some helpful ideas for making the event run smoothly.

● Prepare as many dishes as possible in advance – sauces, salads, desserts, etc.

● Unless you have an extremely large barbecue, it is probably simpler to cook a large quantity of jacket potatoes in the conventional oven.

● Offer nibbles while your guests are enjoying a drink and waiting for the food to be cooked. Sticks of raw vegetables with dips and bowls of olives are ideal appetisers.

● Choose smaller pieces of food for the occasion – small chops, sausages, chicken drumsticks for instance. You will fit more on the barbecue. Kebabs are ideal too, if a little fiddly to prepare.

● Alternatively, you may decide to grill one large item (such as Butterfly Lamb on page 67) and start cooking it before your guests arrive.

● If you have to barbecue in batches, it is probably a good idea to keep the cooked food warm in the conventional oven while the rest is grilled on the barbecue. There is nothing more disconcerting than seeing other guests tucking into delicious food when you have to wait to be served.

● Foods with lengthy cooking times and foods which are suitable for keeping warm should be barbecued first. Leave the quick cooking foods until last. If you plan to serve a quick-cooking starter (such as Garlic Prawns, page 44; Spiced Seafood Kebabs, page 106; or Cheese Bundles, page 102) plan a main course which can be cooked first and kept warm.

● Enlist the help of a friend or family member (in advance) to help carry foods to and from the barbecue and the kitchen, and to heat up dishes like rice and pasta in the microwave.

THEME BARBECUES
Giving a barbecue a theme can create a wonderful atmosphere. Mention the theme to your guests (tailor your invitations accordingly) and they will oblige by dressing appropriately and bringing wine and drink to fit the occasion. Here are some suggestions for putting together eight themes, using recipes from this book with simple salads and breads bought at good supermarkets or speciality shops.

French Barbecue

Starters/Appetisers:
Crudités (small sticks of raw vegetables) with dips
Garlic Prawns, page 44
Mushrooms in Garlic Cheese Sauce, page 122

Main course:
Plain grilled fish or shellfish
Basque Fish Steaks, page 52
Pork with Calvados, page 76
Lemon Herb Steaks, page 57

Salads and vegetables:
Green salad with Basic French Dressing, page 129
Ratatouille Salad, page 139
Marinated Mushrooms, page 137
Grilled vegetables – courgettes, peppers, onions, etc.

Bread:
Crusty French sticks
Garlic Bread, page 145
Garlic Toast, page 145

Dessert:
Normandy Kebabs, page 154
Fresh fruit – cherries, apples, pears, apricots, grapes, etc.
French cheese – Camembert, Brie, etc.

Italian Barbecue

Starters/Appetisers:
Green and black olives
Bread sticks
Grilled sardines

Main course:
Grilled fish or shellfish
Dressed Tuna Steaks, page 50
Veal with Tomato, Mint and Watercress Salad, page 61
Pork and Olive Kebabs, page 101

Salads and vegetables:
Tomato and basil salad with Garlic and Parsley Dressing,
    dressing page 129
Pasta Salad, page 141
Grilled Pepper Salad, page 136
Mediterranean Vegetable Salad, page 142
Grilled vegetables – tomatoes, onions, courgettes,
    peppers, aubergines, etc.

Bread:
Pizza bread or Ciabatta or any crusty bread
Garlic Toast, page 145
Garlic Bread, page 145, made with Tomato Butter, page 148

Dessert:
Fresh fruit salad of orange slices and grapes
Italian ice cream
Italian cheese – such as Dolcelatte

Spanish Barbecue

Starters/Appetisers:
Green and black olives
Tomato and red onion salad or Tomato Salsa, page 60
Grilled sardines

Main Course:
Barbecue Paella, page 48
Spanish Chicken, page 86
Pork and Olive Kebabs, page 101
Grilled fish or shellfish

Salads and vegetables:
Simple Rice Salad, page 134, with peas, peppers and
    cucumber
Grilled Pepper Salad, page 136
Mediterranean Vegetable Salad, page 142
Cucumber Salad, page 138
Spring Kebabs, page 98

Bread:
Any crusty bread

Dessert:
Fresh fruit – oranges, figs, grapes, pomegranates

Chinese Barbecue

Starters/Appetisers:
Prawn Crackers
Barbecued Ribs of Pork, page 72

Main course:
Chinese Chicken Drumsticks, page 93
Chicken Satay, page 108

Chicken in Coconut and Lime, page 89
Thai Beef Steaks, page 58
Pork with Honey and Soy Baste, page 32, and Sweet and
    Sour Sauce, page 39
Oriental Tofu Kebabs, page 103

Salads and vegetables:
Simple Rice Salad, page 134 (add some soy sauce to the
    dressing)
Plain or fried rice or noodles
Salads made with Chinese leaves, beansprouts, bamboo
    shoots, baby corn, spring onions, etc.

Dessert:
Pineapple with Stem Ginger, page 156
Fresh Fruit – lychees, rambutans, kiwi fruit

Indian Barbecue

Starters/Appetisers:
Poppadums with small bowls of lime pickle, Cucumber
    Raita, page 111, Tomato Salsa, page 60, and mango
    chutney

Main course:
Lamb Tikka, page 68
Tandoori Chicken, page 88
Vegetable Skewers with Lentil Dhal, page 104
Spicy Beef Kebabs with Cucumber Raita, page 111
Lamb or Chicken with Eastern Spice Baste, page 33

Salads and vegetables:
Pillau Rice Salad, page 140
Tomato and raw onion salad
Grilled vegetables – aubergines, onions, tomatoes.

Bread:
Naan or chapatis

Dessert:
Fresh fruit – bananas, lychees, rambutans, coconut
Grilled bananas, page 151

African Barbecue

Starters/Appetisers
Small vegetables or lamb on skewers with Eastern
  Spice Baste, page 33

Main Course:
African Lamb, page 70
Moroccan Lamb Kebabs with Minted Yoghurt, page 110
Dusky Chicken with Melon, page 91
Lamb or Chicken with a dry spice marinade, page 31

Salads and vegetables:
Grilled Pepper Salad, page 136
Cucumber Salad, page 138
Peppers with Cracked Wheat Filling, page 125
Grilled Stuffed Aubergines, page 126
Sweetcorn Packets, page 123
Green salad or tomato salad with Mint Dressing, page 130

Bread:
Wholewheat bread

Dessert:
Baked Bananas with Brandy Sauce, page 155
Fresh fruit – mangoes, pawpaw, grapes, oranges, apricots,
  peaches

Scandinavian Barbecue

Starters/Appetisers:
Smoked herrings
Sticks of raw vegetables with a yoghurt dip

Main course:
Barbecue Frikadeller, page 73
Sticky Glazed Bacon, page 79
Cucumber-Stuffed Herrings, page 47
Grilled fish or shellfish

Salads and vegetables:
Marinated Mushrooms, page 137

Red cabbage cooked gently with a cooking apple and a
  few tablespoons of vinegar and sugar
Green salad
Summer Potato Salad, page 133

Bread:
Rye bread and/or wholewheat bread

Dessert:
Fresh fruit with yoghurt – raspberries, blueberries,
  cranberries, grapes
A selection of Danish cheeses

Greek Barbecue

Starters/Appetisers:
Black olives
Cheese Bundles, page 102
Taramasalata with warm pitta bread

Main course:
Lamb with Yoghurt and Herb Baste, page 33
Quick Kofta Kebabs, page 113
Grilled fish with Tomato Sauce, page 37

Salads and vegetables:
Mediterranean Vegetable Salad, page 142
Tomato salad with black olives, pepper, cucumber and
  cubes of Feta cheese
Green salad with Garlic and Parsley Dressing, page 129
Grilled vegetables – aubergines, tomatoes, onions,
  peppers

Bread:
Pitta bread warmed or toasted

Dessert:
Fresh fruit served with yoghurt – melon, grapes, figs
Turkish Delight
Grilled Halloumi or Feta cheese with fresh fruit

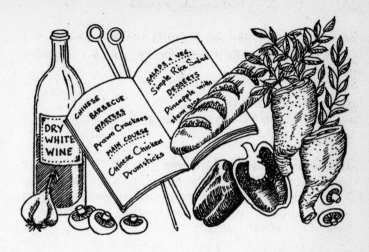

2. ABOUT THE RECIPES

Servings
Most recipes serve between four to eight people. This is
intentional. In my opinion, you are unlikely to barbecue
for fewer than four, and it is often simpler to multiply
recipe ingredients than it is to reduce them.

Ingredients
These are given in metric and imperial for your conven-
ience. Use either one set of measures or the other, do not
mix them in the same recipe. All spoon quantities are
level unless otherwise stated.

Ingredients are generally listed in the order in which
they are used, and the methods are numbered for quick
reference.

Cooking times
Cooking times are approximate only. They will depend on
the starting temperature of the food (remember to allow
refrigerated food to come back to room temperature
before barbecuing), the size and thickness of the food,
and the heat of the coals. As a guide, hold your hand a few
inches (about three) above the coals. If the heat allows

you to keep your hand in position for five seconds, it is
fairly low; 3–4 seconds is medium hot, and 2–3 seconds is
hot.

What to serve with what
You will find helpful serving suggestions at the end of
each recipe method.

Advance preparation and freezing
Also at the end of each recipe are appropriate instructions
for preparing part or all the recipe in advance. In addition,
I have indicated whether the recipe is suitable for
freezing, and at what stage.

From barbecue to grill
You will be pleased to know that all those recipes in 'The
Barbecue Cook' which are suitable for barbecuing, are
also suitable for cooking under a conventional grill. This is
particularly useful if the weather is not as good as you
expected. Remember to pre-heat the grill before cooking
and brush the food with oil, marinade or baste as
instructed in the recipe method.

The microwave
In several recipes I have indicated when a method is
suitable for microwave cooking. When cooking times are
given, these are based on full power (100%) in a 650 Watt
cooker. They are approximate only. Microwave and
combination cookers vary from model to model, so
cooking times will vary too. You will be familiar with your
own cooker and will be able to make adjustments to suit
it.

3. MARINADES AND BASTES

MARINADES

The benefits of marinating food are threefold. Not only is it a convenient way of tenderising meat and poultry, it can also impregnate the food with delicious flavours, while oil-based marinades add moisture and help to protect the food from drying out during cooking on the barbecue.

- It is the acid in a marinade which tenderises. Choose wine, wine vinegar or lemon juice. Yoghurt can be used too.

- Food for barbecuing benefits from the addition of strong flavours – more pungent than you might use for other cooking methods. Mild flavours would be masked by the 'barbecue' flavour. Experiment with herbs, spices, garlic, onions, citrus rinds, and so on.

- Whisk together the marinade ingredients, shake them up in a screw-topped jar, or mix them in a blender or processor.

● Arrange food to be marinated in a single layer.

● Use a non-metallic dish and turn the food in the marinade from time to time.

● Meat and poultry can be marinated for two hours or more, or overnight.

● Fish is generally tender and needs only 30 minutes to one hour for cubed fish, fillets and shellfish; or 2–4 hours for whole fish (depending on its size).

● If you plan to marinate food for more than two hours, keep it refrigerated.

● Remember to allow refrigerated food to come back to room temperature before barbecuing – it will cook more evenly and it will certainly taste better.

● Lift the food out of the marinade and drain it just before cooking.

● Use the rest of the marinade to baste the food during cooking or as the basis for a sauce.

A marinade for fish or vegetables
60ml (4 tbsp) olive oil
Grated rind and juice of 1 lemon
2 spring onions or 1 shallot, finely chopped
1 clove garlic, crushed (optional)
Freshly milled pepper
Sprig parsley
Bay leaf

A marinade for steak
30ml (2 tbsp) sunflower or soya oil
30ml (2 tbsp) dark soy sauce
30ml (2 tbsp) soft brown sugar
60ml (4 tbsp) lemon juice
5ml (1 tsp) root ginger, finely chopped or grated
1 clove garlic, crushed
Freshly milled black pepper

A marinade for pork
60ml (4 tbsp) olive oil
60ml (4 tbsp) white wine or dry cider
Grated rind of 1 orange
2 spring onions, finely chopped
Freshly milled black pepper

A marinade for lamb
75ml (5 tbsp) olive oil
75ml (5 tbsp) red wine
1 small onion, grated
2 sprigs rosemary
Grated rind 1 lemon

A marinade for poultry
30ml (2 tbsp) salad oil
60ml (4 tbsp) dark soy sauce
60ml (4 tbsp) dry sherry
30ml (2 tbsp) clear honey
2.5ml (½ tsp) ground chilli powder
Salt

Traditional Barbecue Sauce Marinade – see page 35

A dry spice marinade
Coats up to 20 pieces of meat, depending on size.

This recipe is a concoction of spices which gives a deliciously warm flavour when rubbed on the surface of lamb, pork, poultry or beef. It will keep indefinitely in an airtight jar, so it can be ready to use all summer.

50g (2 oz) dark brown sugar
15ml (1 tbsp) chilli powder
10ml (2 tsp) ground cinnamon
10ml (2 tsp) ground nutmeg
5ml (1 tsp) ground cumin
2.5ml (½ tsp) ground cloves
2.5ml (½ tsp) cayenne pepper
2.5ml (½ tsp) ground black pepper

Shake all the ingredients together in an airtight jar. To use, rub the spices onto meat surface (sprinkle the meat with a little salt first, if liked), cover and refrigerate overnight.

BASTES

A baste is a sauce which adds flavour to foods and keeps them moist on the barbecue. It is usually made up of strong-flavoured ingredients plus honey or sugar to give a glaze. A baste is brushed onto the food up to an hour before grilling. Keep it beside you while you are cooking too, so that you can baste the food often.

These recipes are all suitable for preparing several hours or a day ahead.

Honey and Soy
Use on vegetables, poultry, pork or lamb.
Mix together:
**60ml (4 tbsp) dark soy sauce (use light soy sauce
   for vegetables)**
30ml (2 tbsp) honey

Add some chopped fresh herbs (tarragon or parsley) or some finely chopped fresh root ginger if liked.

Redcurrant and Vermouth
Use on lamb or on fruit kebabs.
Melt together:

45ml (3 tbsp) redcurrant jelly
15ml (1 tbsp) dry vermouth

Add some finely grated orange rind if liked.

Lime and Ginger
Use on fish.
Mix together:

Grated rind and juice of a lime
15ml (1 tbsp) finely chopped fresh root ginger
30ml (2 tbsp) honey

Yoghurt and Herb
Use on lamb, pork or poultry.
Mix together:

60ml (4 tbsp) natural thick yoghurt
15ml (1 tbsp) lemon juice
15ml (1 tbsp) oil
15ml (1 tbsp) chopped chives
15ml (1 tbsp) chopped parsley, coriander or fennel

Eastern Spice
Use on lamb, pork and poultry.
Mix together:

60ml (4 tbsp) Greek yoghurt
15ml (1 tbsp) olive oil
10ml (2 tsp) soft brown sugar
5ml (1 tsp) ground cumin
5ml (1 tsp) ground coriander
A pinch of cayenne pepper

Orange and Spring Onion
Use on steak, poultry and lamb.
Melt together:

45ml (3 tbsp) orange marmalade
15ml (1 tbsp) white wine

Add 1 spring onion, finely chopped

Tomato and Worcestershire Sauce
Use on sausages, frankfurters, burgers, and poultry.
Mix together:

45ml (3 tbsp) tomato ketchup
15ml (1 tbsp) oil
15ml (1 tbsp) Worcestershire Sauce

Add a dash of hot chilli pepper sauce if liked.

4. SAUCES

An interesting sauce can make the simplest barbecued food into something special. Unless you have a large barbecue, it is not worth trying to prepare it in a pan on the grid.

It is far better to make it ahead of time, along with the salads, so that the cook can concentrate on the rest of the meal.

Simply warm it through, just before serving.

Traditional Barbecue Sauce
Serves 4

Serve this popular sauce with barbecued steaks, chops, hamburgers, sausages, chicken or jacket potatoes.

The cooked sauce can also be used as a marinade for chicken pieces, pork chops or spare ribs (see page 72).

1 onion, chopped very finely
15ml (1 tbsp) oil
60ml (4 tbsp) tomato purée
45ml (3 tbsp) red wine vinegar
30ml (2 tbsp) Worcestershire sauce
30ml (2 tbsp) brown sugar
15ml (1 tbsp) English mustard powder
Salt and black pepper

1. Cook the onion, gently in the oil until very soft but not brown (or microwave for 3 minutes).

2. Stir in the remaining ingredients, plus 150ml (¼ pt) water.

3. Bring to the boil, then cover and simmer for 10 minutes (or microwave for 5 minutes).

● Can be prepared one or two days in advance. Complete steps 1 to 3, cover and refrigerate.

● Suitable for freezing.

St Clements Sauce
Serves 6–8

This light, tangy orange and lemon sauce is ideal for serving with fish, vegetables, poultry or hot rice.

25g (1 oz) butter
1 medium onion, finely chopped
30ml (2 tbsp) plain flour
15ml (1 tbsp) sugar
150ml (¼ pt) vegetable stock
45ml (3 tbsp) dry vermouth
Grated rind and juice of 1 orange
30ml (2 tbsp) lemon juice
Salt and freshly milled pepper
150ml (¼ pt) whipping cream

1. Melt the butter and cook the onion gently until very soft but not brown (or microwave for 3 minutes).

2. Remove from the heat and stir in the flour and sugar. Gradually blend in the vegetable stock and dry vermouth, then add the orange rind and juice and lemon juice.

3. Bring to the boil, stirring continually (or microwave until it boils, stirring frequently). Season to taste with salt and pepper.

4. Stir in the cream and heat gently to serve.

● Can be prepared a day ahead. Complete steps 1–3, cover and refrigerate overnight. Warm through before completing step 4.

● Suitable for freezing after step 3. Thaw completely and warm through before completing step 4.

Tomato Sauce
Serves 4–6

Serve this fresh-tasting sauce with fish, vegetables, meat or poultry. It helps to have a food processor for this recipe.

1 small onion, finely chopped
1 small carrot, finely chopped
1 clove garlic, crushed
15ml (1 tbsp) oil
15ml (1 tbsp) cornflour
398g (14 oz) can chopped tomatoes or 450g (1 lb) fresh ripe tomatoes, skinned and chopped
300ml (½ pt) chicken or vegetable stock
15ml (1 tbsp) sugar
15ml (1 tbsp) tomato purée
Bay leaf
Salt and freshly milled black pepper

1. Cook the onion, carrot and garlic gently in the oil until very soft and light golden brown (or microwave for 3 minutes).

2. Stir in the cornflour, then add the tomatoes and their juice. Stir in the chicken or vegetable stock, sugar, tomato purée and a little seasoning. Bring to the boil, then simmer gently for 20–30 minutes (or microwave for 10 minutes).

3. Blend or process the sauce, then pass it through a sieve to make a smooth seed-free sauce.

4. Adjust seasoning to taste and reheat before serving.

● Can be prepared a day ahead. Complete steps 1–3, cover and refrigerate overnight.

● Suitable for freezing.

Cumberland Sauce
Serves 4

Serve this pretty sauce with hot or cold meats such as ham, venison, lamb or turkey.

1 large orange
Juice of 1 large lemon
75ml (5 tbsp) redcurrant jelly
60ml (4 tbsp) port or red wine
5ml (1 tsp) French mustard
5–10ml (1–2 tsp) arrowroot

1. Pare the rind off the orange with a potato peeler. Cut the rind into very fine strips. Cover with water, bring to the boil and simmer for 10 minutes (or microwave for 5 minutes). Drain and cool.

2. Extract the juice from the orange. In a small pan combine the orange juice with the lemon juice, redcurrant jelly, port or red wine, and mustard. Stir gently over a medium heat (or microwave) until the redcurrant jelly melts. Add the orange rind, bring to the boil then remove from the heat.

3. Mix the arrowroot with sufficient water to make a thin, smooth paste. Stir half of it into the sauce and bring to the boil, stirring. Repeat this process, adding sufficient arrowroot to make a thick, glossy sauce.

● Can be prepared a day ahead. Complete steps 1–3, cover and refrigerate overnight. Reheat gently before serving, thinning the sauce with a little extra water if necessary.

● Suitable for freezing.

Sweet and Sour Sauce
Serves 6–8

This version of 'sweet and sour' is dark, rich and chunky.
Serve it with burgers, pork chops or pork spare ribs.

15ml (1 tbsp) oil
1 onion, sliced
1 clove garlic, crushed (optional)
1 green pepper, sliced
398g (14 oz) can chopped tomatoes
60ml (4 tbsp) red wine vinegar
60ml (4 tbsp) soy sauce
30ml (2 tbsp) cornflour
75g (3 oz) soft brown sugar
2.5ml (½ tsp) mixed dried herbs
220g can pineapple slices in natural juice
Salt and black pepper

1. Heat the oil and cook the onion, garlic and pepper
   until soft (or microwave for 5 minutes). Stir in the
   tomatoes and their juice.

2. Blend the next five ingredients with the pineapple
   juice and top up to 300ml (½ pt) with water.

3. Stir the liquid into the tomatoes. Bring to boil,
   stirring, until the sauce is smooth and glossy, then
   simmer gently for a few minutes (or microwave,
   stirring once or twice, until the sauce is thick, smooth
   and glossy – about 5 minutes).

4. Season to taste with salt and black pepper. Cut the
   pineapple into chunks and stir into the sauce.

● Can be prepared a day ahead. Complete steps 1–4,
  cover and refrigerate overnight.

● Suitable for freezing.

Mushroom Curry Sauce
Serves 4–6

Curry pastes vary in their strength, so adjust the quantity used in this recipe to suit your palate. Serve with poultry, meat, vegetables, or fish; or as a filling for jacket potatoes.

1 medium onion, finely chopped
15ml (1 tbsp) oil
1 clove garlic, crushed
225g (8 oz) cup mushrooms, sliced
1 large eating apple, peeled, cored and chopped
30ml (2 tbsp) curry paste
10ml (2 tsp) chopped root ginger
2.5ml (½ tsp) ground turmeric
300ml (½ pt) vegetable or chicken stock
50g (2 oz) creamed coconut
15ml (1 tbsp) lemon juice
Salt and pepper
150ml (¼ pt) single cream

1. Cook the onion gently in the oil until soft and golden brown (or microwave for 3 minutes).
2. Stir in the garlic, mushrooms, apple, curry paste, root ginger, turmeric, stock and coconut. Bring to the boil, stirring to melt the coconut, then simmer for 10–15 minutes, stirring occasionally (or microwave for 5–8 minutes, stirring once or twice).
3. Add the lemon juice and season to taste with salt and pepper.
4. Stir in the cream and heat through before serving.

● Can be prepared a day ahead. Complete steps 1 and 2, cover and refrigerate overnight. Warm the sauce through before completing steps 3 and 4.

● Suitable for freezing after step 2. Thaw completely and warm through before completing steps 3 and 4.

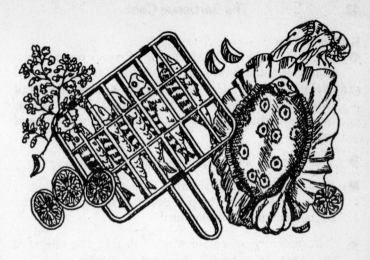

5. FISH AND SHELLFISH

Barbecuing is probably my favourite way of cooking fish. As a family we have had many a happy day grilling fish, fresh from a coastal supply, over a battered portable barbecue on the beach – both at home and in France. Wedges of lemon or lime and some fresh bread were the only extras we required.

I like to prepare fish in the simplest way. Some types have such a delicate flavour, like salmon or bass, that I would not want to mask it with strong herbs or spices. A brushing of melted butter or oil, with a bay leaf and/or lemon wedge inserted in the fish cavity, is sufficient, and delicious. Or try brushing the fish with lemon butter (page 147), herb butter (page 147) or pesto (a basil and olive oil paste). If you want to add flavour to bland white fish, a simple marinade plus the flavour imparted by the smoking barbecue does the trick. Alternatively, cook fish fillets or cutlets in a parcel of buttered, double-thickness foil with a slice of savoury butter, a dash of white wine and some tomato slices or strips of blanched vegetables (courgettes, peppers, celery, carrot, onion, etc.).

Barbecue Tips

- Cook fish whole, in cutlets, or in cubes on skewers. Fillets of fish are best cooked in foil – they break too easily otherwise. Use firm fish for kebabs – cod cut from the thick end of the fillet is suitable, as well as huss, monkfish, tuna, shark, swordfish, scallops and prawns.

- Thaw frozen fish completely before cooking.

- Brush white fish and shellfish with oil or melted butter before grilling – to help prevent it drying out on the barbecue and to add flavour.

- Alternatively, marinate white fish (use the oil-based marinade on page 30). Allow it to marinate for ½–1 hour for cubed fish, fillets and shellfish, or 2–4 hours for whole fish (depending on its size). Baste the fish with the remaining marinade during cooking.

- Slash the skin of whole oily fish in two or three places before grilling – herring and mackerel, for instance.

- Oil the grill rack well before cooking fish. The same goes for hinged wire grids, fish-shaped grids and skewers.

- Turn the fish frequently during grilling – use a long-handled fish slice or, if possible, a hinged wire grid.

- Oily fish, such as mackerel, can cause flare-ups on the barbecue as the oil drips out and ignites on the hot coals. Avoid positioning the cooking grid too near the coals.

- Small oily fish (sardines or sprats) can be cooked without brushing them with oil.

- Fish is delicate and breaks easily. A hinged wire grid is useful for cooking all types of fish, enabling it to be turned over without breaking.

- Cooking times for fish are generally short, so cook it

just before you want to eat it. Cooking times will depend on the size and thickness of the fish and the amount of heat given off by the barbecue. As a general guide:

> *fillets, small whole fish and cubes of fish*: 2–3 minutes each side
> *cutlets, such as cod, salmon*: about 3–4 minutes each side
> *medium whole fish*: 4–8 minutes each side, depending on the size
> *large whole fish, such as bass*: 10–15 minutes each side.

Fish cooked in foil parcels will take slightly longer.

● Avoid overcooking fish or it will lose its flavour and become dry. Test that it is cooked by pushing a knife gently into the flesh: the flakes should be opaque and should move easily away from the bone.

● Serve barbecued fish with lemon or lime wedges, lemon mayonnaise (page 132) or St Clements Sauce (page 36).

Garlic Prawns
Serves 6

Serve these garlicky prawns as a starter. The aroma is wonderful.

100g (4 oz) butter
2 cloves garlic, crushed
30ml (2 tbsp) chopped parsley
10ml (2 tsp) light soy sauce
450g (1 lb) peeled prawns, thawed and drained if frozen

1. Melt the butter and stir in the garlic, parsley and soy sauce.

2. Pour the butter into 6 individual flameproof dishes or foil containers and allow to cool and set.

3. Divide the prawns between the dishes, piling them on top of the set butter. Cover and refrigerate until needed – up to 2 hours.

4. Heat the dishes on the barbecue, over a medium heat until the butter melts and the prawns begin to sizzle.

Serve immediately with small slices of bread to mop up the juices.

Trout with Fennel
Serves 4

The simplest dishes are often the best. If you are unable to buy fennel, use a few sliced celery stalks with some fennel seeds.

1 fennel bulb
30ml (2 tbsp) oil
1 small onion, sliced finely
4 trout, cleaned
Flour seasoned with salt and pepper

1. Trim the fennel and slice thinly.

2. Heat the oil in a pan and cook the fennel and onion gently until very soft (or microwave until soft). Allow to cool.

3. Pile a quarter of the fennel into each trout cavity.

4. Dip the trout into seasoned flour, coating the skin well.

5. Grill over a medium heat for 6–10 minutes, depending on the size of fish. When cooked, the flesh should flake away from the backbone.

Serve with a dressed green salad.
● The stuffing can be prepared up to a day ahead. Complete steps 1 and 2, cover and refrigerate overnight.

Grilled Mackerel with Caraway Seeds
Serves 4

Try using cumin seeds as a change from caraway seeds.

4 mackerel, cleaned
Pepper
2.5–5ml (½–1 tsp) caraway seeds
30ml (2 tbsp) oil
15ml (1 tbsp) lemon juice
1–2 cloves garlic, crushed (optional)

1. Using a sharp knife, make several diagonal slits in each side of the mackerel. Season the fish with pepper, inside and outside. Sprinkle a few caraway seeds into each of the slits.

2. Whisk together the remaining ingredients and brush over the fish.

3. Grill over a high heat for 4–5 minutes on each side, or until cooked through and the skin is blistered and crispy.

Serve with a selection of salads.

Cucumber-Stuffed Herrings
Serves 6

This oily fish makes a light and economical dish. The stuffing complements the fish well. Use a hinged grid for cooking – for easier turning.

50g (2 oz) fresh breadcrumbs
5cm (2 in) piece cucumber, deseeded and chopped
30ml (2 tbsp) chopped chives or spring onion tops
15ml (1 tbsp) tomato purée
15ml (1 tbsp) lemon juice
1 x size 4 egg, beaten
Salt and black pepper
6 boned herring fillets

1. Mix together the breadcrumbs, cucumber and chives. Blend the tomato purée, lemon juice and beaten egg. Mix into the breadcrumbs and season with salt and black pepper.

2. Spread a portion of the stuffing down the centre of each herring fillet. Fold each fillet lengthways, to return it to its 'fish' shape.

3. Cook in an oiled grid for 5–7 minutes each side until the skins are crisp.

Serve as a starter or as a main course with bread spread with Lemon Butter (page 147) and toasted on the barbecue, and salad.

● Can be prepared several hours ahead. Complete steps 1 and 2 and keep refrigerated. Bring back to room temperature before cooking.

Barbecue Paella
Serves 8

I owe the idea for this version of the spectacular Spanish dish to a good friend. The chicken and shellfish are added, hot off the barbecue, to the cooled rice base – ideal for special occasions. Use a risotto rice if you can, long-grain rice if not.

90ml (6 tbsp) olive oil, plus extra for brushing
1 medium onion, finely chopped
2 red peppers, deseeded and sliced
2 cloves garlic, crushed
450g (1 lb) risotto rice
1 litre (1¾ pt) hot vegetable or chicken stock
150ml (¼ pt) white wine
4 tomatoes, skinned and chopped
2.5ml (½ tsp) saffron powder
Salt and freshly milled black pepper
225–350g (8–12 oz) fresh mussels
50g (2 oz) butter, melted
30ml (2 tbsp) chopped parsley
45ml (3 tbsp) lemon juice
20ml (1 good tbsp) clear honey
8 chicken thighs
16 whole prawns
1 large lemon

1. Heat 45ml (3 tbsp) of the oil in a large pan and cook the onion, peppers and garlic until soft but not brown (or microwave for 5 minutes).

2. Stir in the rice then add the hot stock, wine, tomatoes, saffron and seasoning. Bring to the boil, stir, then cover and simmer gently until the rice is tender and the liquid has been absorbed – about 20 minutes. Stir occasionally during cooking. (Alternatively microwave for 10 minutes.) Empty the rice into a large bowl and allow it to cool.

3. Meanwhile, steam the mussels open in a large pan with 1cm (½ inch) boiling water. Drain them and discard any that do not open.

4. Spread the mussels in an even layer on a large square of double-thickness foil. Dribble the melted butter over them and scatter the parsley over. Close the foil parcel and seal it tightly. Refrigerate until needed.

5. Whisk together the remaining 45ml (3 tbsp) olive oil, lemon juice and honey. Pour the dressing over the rice and mix it in gently. Pile into a large, shallow serving dish.

6. Brush the chicken thighs with oil. Grill over a medium heat for 20–25 minutes, turning frequently, until the juices run clear when the pieces are pierced with a skewer. Keep them warm on the side of the barbecue.

7. Brush the prawns with oil and place these alongside the foil parcel of mussels on the barbecue. Grill over a medium heat for 10 minutes (turn the prawns half way, but not the mussels).

8. Tip the mussels and their buttery juices onto the rice and stir in gently. Arrange the chicken and prawns over the top of the rice. Garnish with lemon wedges.

Serve with fresh crusty bread
●   The rice and the mussels can be prepared several hours ahead. Complete steps 1–5. Refrigerate the mussels. Cover and refrigerate the rice if it is prepared more than 2 hours ahead – make sure it returns to room temperature before serving.

Dressed Tuna Steaks
Serves 4

Try this piquant dressing on other firm fish steaks – like swordfish or shark. Use a mixture of green and red salad leaves for the best effect.

120ml (4 fl oz) oil, such as grapeseed
60ml (4 tbsp) white wine vinegar
45ml (3 tbsp) single cream
15ml (1 tbsp) Worcestershire sauce
5ml (1 tsp) wholegrain mustard
5ml (1 tsp) anchovy paste
2.5ml (½ tsp) salt
Freshly milled black pepper
4 tuna steaks 175–225g (6–8 oz) each
Crisp lettuce leaves
30ml (2 tbsp) grated fresh Parmesan cheese

1. Whisk together the oil, wine vinegar, cream, Worcestershire sauce, mustard, anchovy paste, salt and black pepper. Transfer 60ml (4 tbsp) to a small dish and reserve the rest.

2. Brush the tuna steaks with the dressing from the small dish and sprinkle with a little freshly milled black pepper. Grill the steaks over a medium heat for about 10 minutes or until cooked through.

3. Arrange some lettuce leaves on each serving plate. Cut each tuna steak into about 4 pieces and scatter over the lettuce. Whisk up the remaining dressing and drizzle it over the fish and salad. Sprinkle with Parmesan cheese and serve.

Serve with vegetable kebabs or warm crusty bread.
● The dressing can be prepared up to a day ahead. Complete step 1, cover and refrigerate overnight. Bring back to room temperature before cooking.

Fish Cakes
Makes 8

They are enjoyed by adults and children alike. I prepare them very simply – if you wish, coat them in egg and breadcrumbs at the end of step 3.

25g (1 oz) butter
1 small onion, finely chopped
200g can tuna in brine, drained; or 175–225g (6–8 oz) smoked mackerel
450g (1 lb) cooked potatoes, mashed
30ml (2 tbsp) chopped parsley
30ml (2 tbsp) tomato purée
15ml (1 tbsp) lemon rind
15ml (1 tbsp) lemon juice
1 egg, beaten
Salt and freshly milled black pepper
Oil for brushing

1. Melt the butter and cook the onion until soft and golden brown (or microwave for 3 minutes).
2. Flake the tuna or mackerel and work it into the mashed potato with the onion and butter, parsley, tomato purée, lemon rind, lemon juice, beaten egg and seasoning.
3. Divide the mixture and shape into 8 balls. Flatten each one into a fish cake shape. Cover and chill for an hour or two to firm up.
4. Brush the fish cakes with oil and grill them on an oiled rack over a medium heat for about 3–5 minutes each side until brown and crispy.

Serve as they are with salads or with a hot sauce such as Tomato Sauce (page 37) or Traditional Barbecue Sauce (page 35).

● Can be prepared a day ahead. Complete steps 1–3, cover and refrigerate overnight.
● Suitable for freezing after stage 3. Thaw completely before cooking.

Basque Fish Steaks
Serves 6

My family and I were served this dish with tuna in a restaurant in St Jean de Luz, on the south-west coast of France. It has adapted well to cooking on the barbecue.

1 large onion, sliced
30ml (2 tbsp) olive oil
2 cloves garlic, crushed
2 red peppers, deseeded and sliced thinly
398g (14 oz) can chopped tomatoes
150ml (¼ pt) red wine
15ml (1 tbsp) sugar
15ml (1 tbsp) fresh thyme leaves or 5ml (1 tsp) dried
30ml (2 tbsp) chopped fresh parsley
Salt and freshly milled black pepper
6 firm fish steaks, such as tuna, shark or swordfish

1. Cook the onion in the oil until soft and pale golden brown. Stir in the garlic and peppers and cook gently for a few minutes (or microwave for 5 minutes).
2. Add the tomatoes, red wine, sugar, herbs and seasoning and bring to the boil. Simmer gently for about 5 minutes (or microwave for 3–5 minutes), then allow the sauce to cool completely.
3. Pour the cold sauce over the tuna steaks and allow them to marinate, covered, for 1–2 hours.
4. Lift the steaks out of the marinade and drain them. Grill over a medium heat for 10–15 minutes until cooked through. Brush the fish with the marinade once or twice during cooking.
5. While the tuna cooks, heat the marinade in a pan until it boils.

Serve each tuna steak with a spoonful of sauce. Accompany it with crusty French bread or plain boiled rice.

● The sauce can be prepared a day ahead. Complete steps 1 and 2, cover and refrigerate overnight.
● The sauce is suitable for freezing after step 2.

6. MEAT

The distinctive flavour of meat cooked on the barbecue is one most of us recognise and enjoy. Those of you who barbecue on a regular basis will know that it can be made even more special with the addition of an interesting marinade. A well-flavoured marinade actually improves the lean cuts of meat we are buying today. Try those featured on pages 30/31 and follow the tips below for succulent results. The recipes are a selection which have been well tested on friends and family over the years.

Barbecue tips
● Always use good quality, tender meat for barbecuing. Choose the cuts you would normally use for roasting, grilling or frying. As a general guide, choose:

Beef – lean steaks (fillet, sirloin, rump, T-bone), good-quality stewing steak (for marinating for kebabs).

Veal – chops, leg fillet, escallop (for kebabs)

Lamb – chops (loin, chump), leg steaks, fillet (for kebabs), liver and kidney (for kebabs)

Pork – chops (loin, spare-rib), spare-ribs, steaks, fillet (for kebabs)

Bacon – chops, gammon steaks, rashers

Sausages, frankfurters and hamburgers – any type

● Trim off excess fat – a lot of dripping fat creates flames, or flare-ups, on the barbecue. If they do occur, use a water spray to control them.

● Marinating meat helps to tenderise it, enhances its flavour, and helps to keep it moist and succulent on the barbecue. See page 30/31 for marinades.

● Make two or three cuts into the fat edge of steaks and gammon to prevent them from curling on the barbe-cue.

● Trim the bone end of chops so that they are easy to pick up with the fingers.

● Oil the barbecue grid and hinged wire grid or skewers, if using them.

● A hinged wire grid makes for easy turning of burgers and sausages, and large numbers of chops or small steaks.

● Cook meat over a high heat to seal it first, then over a medium heat until it is cooked to your liking. Cooking times will depend on the type of meat and its quality, its thickness, and the heat of the barbecue. Here is a general guide:

Steaks – 4–7 minutes each side, depending on how well cooked you want them to be. T-bone steaks need 7–8 minutes each side.

Veal – 8–10 minutes each side (chops), about 4 minutes each side (leg fillet/escallop)

Lamb – 5–8 minutes on each side so that it is brown on the outside and slightly pink on the inside.

Lamb liver, cut into steaks – about 4–5 minutes on each side.

Lamb kidney – about 5 minutes on each side (on kebabs).

Pork and bacon must be well cooked throughout, about 10–12 minutes each side (chops), 25 minutes (cubed on kebabs), 8–10 minutes each side (gammon), 2–3 minutes each side (rashers).

Sausages – 15–20 minutes (large), 10–15 minutes (small chipolata). Long, curled sausages, such as Cumberland will take a little longer.

Frankfurters – these are cooked already and only need heating through.

Hamburgers – 5–10 minutes each side, depending on the thickness.

Steak with Juniper Marinade
Serves 4

The adults in your party will love the unusual flavour of juniper berries. Buy these from good supermarkets and health food stores. This mixture is delicious on pork steaks too.

15ml (1 tbsp) juniper berries
5ml (1 tsp) black peppercorns
2.5ml (½ tsp) salt
2.5ml (½ tsp) mustard power
15–30ml (1–2 tbsp) oil
4 pieces rump steak, about 175–225g (5–8 oz) each

1. Grind the first four ingredients (using a pestle and mortar, liquidiser or processor). Mix in sufficient oil to make a smooth, thick paste.

2. Spread or rub the paste over both sides of each steak. Cover and marinate for 2 hours or more.

3. Grill over a high heat for 5 minutes each side or until the steaks are cooked to your liking.

Serve with a crisp green salad and Spring Kebabs (page 98)

● Can be prepared a day ahead. Complete steps 1 and 2, cover and refrigerate overnight. Bring back to room temperature before cooking.

Lemon Herb Steaks
Serves 8

Carve these steaks into strips before serving on a bed of crisp lettuce. Use a mixture of green and red salad leaves for the most elegant result.

8 sirloin or fillet steaks
120ml (4 fl oz) fresh lemon juice
30ml (2 tbsp) oil
30ml (2 tbsp) fresh thyme leaves
30ml (2 tbsp) fresh rosemary leaves
15ml (1 tbsp) freshly milled black pepper
10ml (2 tsp) grated lemon rind
2.5ml (½ tsp) salt
Crisp lettuce leaves

1. Arrange the steaks in a shallow, non-metallic dish.
2. Whisk the remaining ingredients (except the lettuce) until smooth. Pour over the steaks in the non-metallic dish, cover and marinate for 2 hours or more, turning the steaks over occasionally.
3. Lift the steaks out of the dish, reserving the marinade.
4. Grill over a medium-high heat for about 7 minutes each side or until the steaks are cooked to your liking. Allow the steaks to stand for 5–10 minutes before carving.
5. Meanwhile heat the marinade in a small pan on the side of the barbecue. Bring it to the boil and keep warm.
6. Carve the steaks diagonally into strips, arrange them individually on a bed of crisp lettuce with the hot marinade drizzled over.

Serve with buttered rice or pasta, or Summer Potato Salad (page 133).
● Can be prepared a day ahead. Complete steps 1 and 2, cover and refrigerate overnight. Bring back to room temperature before cooking.

Thai Beef Steaks
Serves 4

Here is another dish which looks more attractive when sliced diagonally into strips before arranging on the serving plate.

45ml (3 tbsp) peanut, walnut or hazelnut oil
Grated rind and juice of one small lime
2 cloves garlic, crushed
4 sirloin or fillet steaks
150ml (¼ pt) vegetable or chicken stock
60ml (4 tbsp) crunchy peanut butter
30ml (2 tbsp) dark soy sauce
15ml (1 tbsp) chopped root ginger
2.5ml (½ tsp) chilli powder, or 1 red chilli, finely chopped
5ml (1 tsp) sugar

1. Whisk together the oil, lime rind and juice, and garlic.
2. Arrange the steaks in a shallow, non-metallic dish and pour the marinade over. Cover and marinate for 2 hours or more, turning the steaks over occasionally.
3. Remove the steaks, reserving the marinade. Keep the steaks covered.
4. Mix the marinade with the remaining ingredients and pour into a small saucepan. Bring to the boil and simmer gently (or microwave) until the sauce thickens.
5. Grill the steaks over a medium-high heat for about 7 minutes each side or until the steaks are cooked to your liking. Allow to stand for 5–10 minutes.
6. Slice the steaks diagonally into strips and arrange on serving plates with a pool of peanut sauce.

Serve with hot noodles tossed in a little nut oil – the one used in the marinade.

● Can be prepared a day ahead. Complete steps 1 and 2, cover and refrigerate overnight. Bring back to room temperature before cooking. Steps 3 and 4 can be completed 2–3 hours ahead.

Steak Burgers
Makes 4 large

Make your own delicious burgers using lean meat with a light seasoning of salt and freshly milled black pepper. Let the toppings add the interest.

700g (1½ lb) rump steak
Salt and freshly milled black pepper

1. Mince or process the steak and season well.

2. Shape into four burgers.

3. Grill over a high heat for 5 minutes each side or until they are cooked to your liking. Use a well-oiled, hinged grid if you have one.

Serve, topped with the dressing of your choice. Choose from the flavoured mayonnaise ideas on page 132 or from those below.
● Can be prepared a day ahead. Complete steps 1 and 2, cover and refrigerate overnight. Bring back to room temperature before cooking.

● Can be frozen. Allow to thaw completely before cooking.

With Roquefort Dressing
Dresses 4–6 burgers

175g (6 oz) Roquefort cheese
15ml (1 tbsp) olive oil
30ml (2 tbsp) chopped chives

Blend the ingredients together well and heat gently in a small pan on the edge of the barbecue.

With Tomato Salsa
Dresses 8 burgers

450g (1 lb) ripe tomatoes, skinned and deseeded
Half a cucumber
1 bunch spring onions, chopped
30–45ml (2–3 tbsp) chopped fresh herbs, such as parsley or
**   mint**
45ml (3 tbsp) olive oil
15ml (1 tbsp) lemon juice
Salt and freshly milled black pepper

Chop the tomato flesh and roughly grate the cucumber
(do not remove the skin). Toss all the ingredients together
in a bowl. Cover and allow to stand until needed.

With Garlic and Herb Cheese
Dresses 6–8 burgers

225g (8 oz) cream cheese
1–2 cloves garlic, crushed
15ml (1 tbsp) each of fresh chopped chives, parsley and
**   tarragon**
45ml (3 tbsp) whipping cream
5ml (1 tsp) lemon juice
Salt and freshly milled black pepper

Blend all the ingredients together and allow to stand for at
least 30 minutes before serving.

With Avocado and Red Onion
Dresses 6 burgers

1 ripe avocado, peeled and stoned
5ml (1 tsp) lemon juice
1 small clove garlic, crushed
Few drops hot chilli sauce
1 small red onion, chopped

Mash the avocado with the lemon juice, garlic and chilli
sauce. Fold in the onion.

Veal with Tomato, Mint and Watercress Salad
Serves 4

The origins of this recipe are Italian. It is just as nice using pork chops.

60ml (4 tbsp) olive oil
30ml (2 tbsp) red wine vinegar
2 cloves garlic, crushed
2 pinches dried thyme
4 veal chops
1 bunch watercress
2 large ripe tomatoes

Salad dressing:
45ml (3 tbsp) olive oil
15ml (1 tbsp) red wine vinegar
60ml (4 tbsp) chopped fresh mint or basil
Salt and freshly milled black pepper

1. Whisk the first four ingredients together. Place the veal in a shallow, non-metallic dish and pour the mixture over it. Cover and marinate for 2 hours, turning the chops once or twice.

2. Trim the watercress, removing tough stems. Wash it and pat it dry. Halve and deseed the tomatoes and cut them into strips. Pile the watercress and tomatoes into a serving bowl.

3. Beat together the ingredients for the salad dressing. Set aside until needed.

4. Drain the veal steaks and grill them over a medium heat for about 8 minutes each side, basting with the marinade, until cooked.

5. Meanwhile, pour the mint/basil dressing over the

watercress and tomatoes and toss them gently.

Serve the veal topped with a mound of the dressed salad. Accompany it with an Italian bread such as Ciabatta (warmed on the barbecue if there is room).

● The veal and salad dressing can be prepared up to a day ahead. Complete steps 1 and 3, cover and refrigerate overnight. Bring back to room temperature before cooking/serving.

Veal Grills with Mushroom Cream Sauce
Serves 4

A quick yet impressive dish for a special occasion. You will need some wooden cocktail sticks. Soak them in water for an hour before use so they don't burn.

4 veal escallops
175g (6 oz) Gruyère cheese
4 thin slices smoked ham
15g (½ oz) butter
100g (4 oz) button mushrooms, sliced
4 spring onions, chopped
150ml (¼ pt) white wine
150ml (¼ pt) whipping cream
Oil
Salt and freshly ground black pepper
Chopped parsley

1. Place the veal between two sheets of clear film or greaseproof paper and beat it with a rolling pin until each piece is about 6mm (¼ in) thick.

2. Cut the cheese into four fingers and wrap each one in a slice of smoked ham. Place a roll of cheese and ham in the centre of each slice of veal. Fold the veal in half and secure the curved edges with a wooden cocktail stick (soaked for an hour in water first).

3. Melt the butter and cook the mushrooms and onions until soft. Add the wine and bring to the boil. Simmer uncovered until the liquid has reduced by half. Stir in the cream and simmer for a few more minutes.

4. Brush the veal with oil and season lightly with salt and freshly ground black pepper.

5. Grill over a medium-high heat for a few minutes on each side, until the veal is cooked and the cheese has

melted inside.

6. Warm the sauce if necessary and serve with the veal grills. Sprinkle with a little chopped parsley.

Serve with green salad and Garlic Toast (page 145).

●   The veal and sauce can be prepared up to a day ahead. Complete steps 1–3, cover and refrigerate overnight. Bring back to room temperature before cooking.

Orange-Glazed Lamb Riblets
Serves 4

The lamb is partially cooked before marinating – for a more tender result. Choose lean ribs to prevent flare-ups on the barbecue.

0.9–1.1kg (2–2½ lb) lean lamb breast riblets
75ml (5 tbsp) orange marmalade
30ml (2 tbsp) wine vinegar
30ml (2 tbsp) soy sauce
10ml (2 tsp) mustard powder

1. Boil the lamb riblets in plenty of water for 15–20 minutes. (Alternatively, microwave on full power (100%) for 3 minutes, then on medium power (50%) for 15 minutes.) Drain well.

2. Place the lamb in a non-metallic dish. Blend together the remaining ingredients and pour over the lamb. Turn them over to coat them well. Allow to cool, cover and refrigerate for 1 hour or more.

3. Grill over a medium heat for about 20 minutes or until crisp, brown and cooked through. Turn them frequently, basting with any extra marinade during cooking.

Serve as a starter or with Simple Rice Salad (page 134).
● Can be prepared a day ahead. Complete steps 1 and 2, cover and refrigerate overnight. Bring back to room temperature before cooking.

Lamb Cutlets with Mustard Cream Sauce
Serves 4

In this recipe the marinade is reduced, then cream is added to make the most delicious sauce.

150ml (¼ pt) white wine
45ml (3 tbsp) wholegrain mustard
45ml (3 tbsp) chopped fresh herbs, such as marjoram or thyme
Salt and black pepper
8 lamb cutlets
150ml (5 fl oz) carton double cream

1. Whisk together the wine, mustard, herbs and seasoning. Place the lamb cutlets in a non-metallic dish and pour the mixture over them. Cover and refrigerate for 2 hours or more.

2. Lift the cutlets out of the marinade.

3. Make the sauce – either use a small robust pan on the barbecue or make the sauce in the kitchen just before grilling the chops (warm it up on the barbecue before serving). Bring the marinade to the boil and simmer until it has reduced by about half. Stir in the cream and adjust seasoning to taste.

4. Grill the cutlets over a medium heat for about 20 minutes, turning occasionally.

Serve with crusty bread and Grilled Pepper Salad (page 136).
● Can be prepared a day ahead. Complete step 1, cover and refrigerate overnight. Bring cutlets back to room temperature before cooking.

Butterfly Lamb
Serves 8

Try this in place of a Sunday roast. Ask your butcher to bone a leg of lamb and open it out into a butterfly shape.

1.8kg (4 lb) leg lamb, boned
Juice 1 lemon
30ml (2 tbsp) olive oil
Freshly ground black pepper
2–3 cloves garlic, peeled and cut into slivers
3–4 sprigs fresh rosemary
30ml (2 tbsp) clear honey

1. Open out the lamb to make a butterfly shape. If there are any very thick areas, beat them flatter with the end of a rolling pin. Trim off any excess fat.
2. Mix together the lemon juice and olive oil and brush some over the cut side of the meat. Season with black pepper.
3. Turn the lamb over, cut side down, and make several deep slits in the top surface with a sharp knife. Insert a sliver of garlic into each. Break up the rosemary sprigs into smaller pieces and insert these too. Brush liberally with the lemon and oil mix and sprinkle with black pepper. Cover and refrigerate for 2 hours or more.
4. Grill over a medium heat for 1–1½ hours, turning occasionally, depending on the thickness of the lamb and how well done you prefer it to be. Ten-to-fifteen minutes before the end of cooking, brush the lamb with the clear honey.

Serve with minted new potatoes or Summer Potato Salad (page 133) and a green salad or Mediterranean Vegetable Salad (see page 142).
● Can be prepared a day ahead. Complete steps 1–3, cover and refrigerate overnight. Bring back to room temperature before cooking.

Lamb Tikka
Serves 8

Lamb is delicious marinaded in a simple mixture of yoghurt, spices and lemon juice.

300ml (½ pt) thick natural yoghurt
5ml (1 tsp) chilli powder
5ml (1 tsp) ground turmeric
5ml (1 tsp) ground coriander
2.5ml (½ tsp) ground ginger
2.5ml (½ tsp) paprika
2 garlic cloves, crushed
30ml (2 tbsp) lemon juice
8 lamb chops, such as chump or leg, weighing 175–225g
   (6–8 oz) each
Lemon wedges

1. Blend together all the ingredients, except the lamb and lemon wedges.

2. Place the lamb chops in a non-metallic dish. Pour the yoghurt marinade over the chops, turning them to make sure they are well coated. Cover and refrigerate for two hours or more.

3. Grill the chops over a medium heat for 20–30 minutes, turning them occasionally, until they are cooked to your liking. Brush with any remaining marinade during cooking.

4. Garnish with lemon wedges.

Serve with Pillau Rice Salad (page 140).
● Can be prepared a day ahead. Complete steps 1 and 2, cover and refrigerate overnight. Bring back to room temperature before cooking.

Curried Lamb Burgers
Makes 6

I like to serve these burgers in warmed pitta bread with tomato salsa and mango chutney.

1 medium onion, finely chopped
15ml (1 tbsp) oil
30ml (2 tbsp) hot curry paste
450g (1 lb) lean lamb, minced
5ml (1 tsp) salt
Freshly milled black pepper
125g (4 oz) fresh breadcrumbs
15ml (1 tbsp) chopped fresh mint
15ml (1 tbsp) chopped fresh coriander or parsley
15ml (1 tbsp) lemon juice
1 egg, beaten

1. Cook the onion in the oil until soft and golden brown (or microwave for 3 minutes).

2. Add the curry paste and allow to cool.

3. Mix the onion into the minced lamb with the remaining ingredients.

4. Divide into six portions and shape into burgers. Cover and chill until needed.

5. Grill over a medium heat (use an oiled, hinged grid if possible) for about 5 minutes each side, or until the lamb is cooked to your liking.

Serve topped with Tomato Salsa (page 60) – try adding a little chopped green chilli to pep it up.

● Can be prepared a day ahead. Complete steps 1–4, cover and refrigerate overnight. Bring back to room temperature before cooking.

● Suitable for freezing. Complete steps 1–4 then freeze. Allow to thaw completely before cooking.

African Lamb
Serves 4

Marinated lamb chops are served together with skewered onions and apricots, and a smooth tomato-based sauce. Just a hint of spice complements the lovely warm colours of this dish. It helps to have a food processor for this recipe.

15ml (1 tbsp) mild curry powder
15ml (1 tbsp) soft brown sugar
5ml (1 tsp) turmeric
30ml (2 tbsp) apricot jam
125ml (4 fl oz) red wine vinegar
4 lamb shoulder chops
8 whole, ready-to-eat dried apricots
8 small, whole onions, peeled
398g (14 oz) can tomatoes
Salt and pepper

1. Blend the curry powder, sugar and turmeric into the apricot jam. Stir in the red wine vinegar plus 125ml (4 fl oz) water.

2. Place the lamb chops in a non-metallic dish, pour the marinade over them, cover and refrigerate for one hour or more.

3. Pour boiling water over the apricots and allow them to plump up for about 10 minutes.

4. Meanwhile, drop the onions into boiling water for 2 minutes, then drain them. (Alternatively, microwave with 30ml (2 tbsp) water for 1½–2 minutes.)

5. Lift the lamb out of its marinade. Thread the apricot and onions alternately onto four skewers and brush them with the marinade.

6. Liquidise or process the remaining marinade with the tomatoes and bring to the boil in a pan. Simmer gently for 10–15 minutes with the lid off. Adjust seasoning if necessary. Keep warm.

7. Grill the chops and kebabs over a medium heat for 15–20 minutes. Move the skewers to a cooler area of the barbecue if they cook too quickly.

Serve the lamb and skewers with a pool of sauce.
●   The lamb can be prepared a day ahead. Complete steps 1 and 2, cover and refrigerate overnight. Bring back to room temperature before cooking.

Barbecued Ribs of Pork
Serves 4

No barbecue book would be complete without this dish. No doubt there will be plenty of finger licking – so hand round the serviettes.

1.4kg (3 lb) lean pork ribs
1 quantity Traditional Barbecue Sauce (see page 35)

1. Arrange the pork ribs in a shallow, non-metallic dish and coat them with the cooled barbecue sauce. Cover and refrigerate for at least 2 hours.

2. Grill the ribs over a medium heat for 30–40 minutes, turning frequently.

3. If wished, boil up any remaining marinade to serve with the ribs.

Serve them just as they are, followed by a variety of salads.
● Can be prepared a day ahead. Complete step 1, cover and refrigerate. Bring back to room temperature before cooking.

Barbecue Frikadeller
Serves 4

This recipe is based on Denmark's national dish. Frying is the usual cooking method, but barbecuing adds that unique flavour. You need a food processor for this recipe.

375g (12 oz) lean minced pork
1 small onion, chopped
Black pepper
2.5ml (½ tsp) salt
2.5ml (½ tsp) ground allspice or nutmeg (optional)
1 egg, size 3 or 4, beaten
45ml (3 tbsp) self-raising flour
30ml (2 tbsp) milk

1. Put the pork, onion, seasonings and spice into a food processor and process into a paste.

2. Blend in the remaining ingredients and shape into four large, or eight small, burgers. Don't worry if the shapes are irregular – they will be more authentic!

3. Grill over a medium heat for 20–30 minutes or until cooked through.

Serve with pickled red cabbage or Tomato Sauce (page 37) and new potatoes with Mustard and Chive Dressing (page 129).
● Can be prepared a day ahead. Complete steps 1 and 2, cover and refrigerate overnight. Bring back to room temperature before cooking.

Pork Chops with Fruit Pockets
Serves 4

Pine kernels and apricots provide the filling, while orange and honey are the main flavours in the marinade. If you cannot get pine kernels, use roughly chopped almonds instead. You will need some wooden cocktail sticks. Soak them in water for an hour before use so they don't burn.

Stuffing:
15g (½ oz) pine kernels
15ml (1 tbsp) oil
1 small onion, sliced finely
25g (1 oz) fresh breadcrumbs
50g (2 oz) ready-to-eat, no-soak dried apricots, chopped
Salt and black pepper

4 pork loin chops
45ml (3 tbsp) oil
30ml (2 tbsp) clear honey
Grated rind 1 orange and 15ml (1 tbsp) orange juice
Black pepper

1. Dry fry the pine kernels in a small frypan until golden brown. Lift out.

2. In the same pan heat the oil and cook the onion until soft and golden brown (or microwave for 3 minutes). Remove from the heat, stir in the breadcrumbs, apricots and pine kernels. Season with salt and black pepper. Allow to cool.

3. Place the tip of a sharp knife as far as you can into the fat edge of the pork chops and cut lengthways along the fat to make a pocket in each. Fill the pockets with the cooled stuffing and close the edges by securing with a wooden cocktail stick (soaked in water for an hour first) or a small metal skewer.

4. Mix together the remaining ingredients. Place the chops in a non-metallic dish and pour the mixture over them. Cover and refrigerate for 2 hours or more.

5. Grill the chops over a medium heat for about 25 minutes, turning occasionally and brushing with extra marinade.

Serve with simple accompaniments, such as a green salad and new potatoes which have been boiled, brushed with oil, threaded on skewers and browned quickly on the barbecue.

● Can be prepared a day ahead. Complete steps 1–4 and refrigerate. Bring back to room temperature before cooking.

Pork with Calvados   *Serves 4*

Calvados (French brandy made with apples) is delicious
with pork. Here, the pork is marinated, then the marinade
is made into a creamy smooth sauce.

15ml (1 tbsp) oil
30ml (2 tbsp) cider vinegar
2.5ml (½ tsp) ground cloves
15ml (1 tbsp) soft brown sugar
45ml (3 tbsp) Calvados or brandy
2 eating apples
4 pork steaks or pork chops
1 small onion, thinly sliced
150ml (5 fl oz) double cream
Salt and black pepper

1. Blend together the oil, vinegar, cloves, sugar and
   Calvados or brandy.
2. Core the apples and cut each one into eight segments.
3. Coat the pork and the apple pieces in the marinade,
   cover and refrigerate for 2 hours or more.
4. Lift the pork and apple pieces out of the marinade.
   Thread the apple pieces onto skewers for easy grilling.
5. In a small covered pan, simmer the onion and the
   marinade with 75ml (3 fl oz) water until the onion is
   soft. With the lid off, boil the sauce to reduce it by
   about half. Stir in the cream then liquidise or sieve it
   to make a smooth sauce. Return the sauce to the pan
   and heat gently before serving. Season to taste with
   salt and pepper.
6. Grill the pork over a medium heat for about 25
   minutes or until cooked through, turning occasionally. Grill the apple for about 10 mintues until golden
   brown.

Serve the pork garnished with golden apple wedges and
the creamy sauce.
● Can be prepared a day ahead. Complete steps 1–3,
   cover and refrigerate overnight. Bring back to room
   temperature before cooking.

Pork with Fennel and Parsley Stuffing
Serves 8

Use a loin of pork and cook it in one piece to create a splendid centre-piece for a 'Sunday Roast' barbecue. Ask your butcher to chine the joint (i.e. remove the backbone). For a quicker version, use thick pork chops, make a pocket in each (see Pork Chops with Fruit Pockets, page 74) to contain the stuffing.

25g (1 oz) butter
1 medium onion, chopped
1 clove garlic, crushed
2 stalks celery, finely chopped
5ml (1 tsp) fennel seeds
45ml (3 tbsp) chopped parsley
40g (1½ oz) fresh breadcrumbs
Salt and freshly milled black pepper
1 lean loin of pork, with 8 chops, chined
Oil for brushing.

1. Melt the butter and cook the onion, garlic, and celery until soft and pale golden brown (or microwave for 3–5 minutes). Stir in the fennel seed, parsley, breadcrumbs and seasoning and allow to cool.

2. Meanwhile score the pork rind with a sharp knife if this has not already been done. Make a cut into the narrow side of the joint to run parallel with the bones (see illustration overleaf).

3. Push the stuffing into the pocket, spreading it evenly, then close and secure it with one or two small metal skewers.

4. Brush the joint with oil and grill over a medium heat for 1–1½ hours, turning occasionally, until cooked through. The meat juices should run clear when the thickest part of the joint is pierced with a knife or skewer.

Carve between the bones to give eight servings. Serve
with Marinated Mushrooms (page 137) and Grilled Pepper
Salad (page 136).
● Can be cooked a day in advance and served cold
with a selection of salads.

Sticky Glazed Bacon
Serves 8

Children in particular love the sticky, sweet-and-sour glaze and it couldn't be easier to prepare. Try it on sausages and beefburgers too.

60ml (4 tbsp) ginger preserve
60ml (4 tbsp) tomato ketchup
15ml (1 tbsp) Worcestershire Sauce
8 bacon chops

1. Blend the ginger preserve, tomato ketchup and Worcestershire sauce well.

2. Spread the glaze over the chops, making sure they are well coated. Cover and refrigerate for one hour or more.

3. Grill the chops over a medium heat for 20–25 minutes, turning frequently and basting with any remaining glaze.

Serve in crusty bread or with jacket potatoes and salad.
● Can be prepared a day ahead. Complete steps 1 and 2, cover and refrigerate overnight.

Bacon and Apple Burgers
Makes 4–6

In these burgers, bacon and apple marry well to give a light, yet tasty combination. You need a food processor for this recipe.

15ml (1 tbsp) oil
1 onion, chopped finely
1 clove garlic, crushed
450g (1 lb) piece lean bacon
1 eating apple
25g (1 oz) breadcrumbs
15ml (1 tbsp) chopped sage, or 5ml (1 tsp) dried
1 egg yolk
Black pepper

1. Heat the oil in a small pan and soften the onion and garlic without browning (or microwave for three minutes). Allow to cool.

2. Mince or process the bacon.

3. Peel, core and grate the apple.

4. Mix the onion, bacon and apple with the breadcrumbs, sage and egg yolk. Season with black pepper. Divide the mixture into four or six portions and shape into burgers.

5. Grill over a medium heat for 20–30 minutes or until cooked through, turning them often.

Serve in soft rolls with crisp lettuce and tomato slices, or with jacket potatoes and green salad.
● Can be prepared a day ahead. Complete steps 1–4, cover and refrigerate overnight. Bring back to room temperature before cooking.

Gammon with Mustard, Honey and Ginger
Serves 4

The marinade imparts a delicious sweet-and-sour flavour
to the gammon slices.

15ml (1 tbsp) oil
15ml (1 tbsp) red wine vinegar
30ml (2 tbsp) clear honey
30ml (2 tbsp) wholegrain mustard
2.5cm (1 in) piece root ginger, grated
4 gammon steaks

1. Mix together the first five ingredients in a shallow,
    non-metallic dish.

2. Snip the fatty edges of the gammon steaks to prevent
    them curling up during cooking. Turn the steaks over
    in the marinade to coat them well. Cover and
    refrigerate for 2 hours or more.

3. Grill over a medium heat for 10–15 minutes, turning
    occasionally and basting with extra marinade.

Serve with Simple Rice Salad (page 134), Spring Kebabs
(page 98) or Summer Potato Salad (page 133).
● Can be prepared a day ahead. Complete steps 1 and
   2, cover and refrigerate overnight. Bring back to
   room temperature before cooking.

Crispy Sausage Fingers
Serves 4

These are ideal for chilly winter evenings – Halloween or Guy Fawkes' night for instance. My teenage tasters loved them!

280g packet bread mix
Oil
40ml (8 tsp) Dijon mustard
225g (8 oz) Gouda cheese, grated
8 small smoked sausages, such as kabanas, or cooked sausages of your choice

1. Make up the bread mix according to pack instructions, adding 15ml (1 tbsp) oil to the mix. Divide it into eight balls. Roll them out into thin ovals, slightly wider than the length of the sausages, and about 20cm (8 in) long.

2. Spread 5ml (1 tsp) mustard on each oval. Sprinkle the cheese over the mustard, dividing it equally. Place a sausage across one end of each oval and roll them up. Pinch the edges to seal them.

3. Brush with oil before and during grilling over a medium heat for about 15 minutes. The bread casing should be cooked through.

Serve just as they are, held in a paper napkin. Offer extra mustard or relishes if wished.
●   Can be prepared up to a day ahead. Complete steps 1 and 2, cover and refrigerate. Bring back to room temperature before cooking.

Sausage Sizzlers
Serves 4–8

The traditional marriage of pork and fruit is used here, with a crispy bacon wrapping – another good choice for cold winter evenings. You will need some wooden cocktail sticks. Soak them in water for an hour before use so they don't burn.

8 large pork sausages
1 large eating apple or 24 no-soak, ready-to-eat dried apricots
8 rashers rindless streaky bacon

1. Use a sharp knife to make a lengthways slit in each sausage – not quite all the way through.

2. Core the apple, if using, and cut into eight wedges. Push one apple wedge (skin-side out), or 3 apricots into each sausage. Use your hands to close the sausage around the fruit.

3. Stretch the bacon rashers with the back of a knife. Wrap one rasher around each sausage and secure with a wooden cocktail stick (soak the sticks in water for 1 hour before use).

4. Grill over a medium heat, turning frequently, for about 20 minutes.

Serve with fresh, crusty rolls, or simply hand-held in a napkin. They are good with Tomato Sauce too (page 37).
● Can be prepared a day ahead. Complete steps 1–3, cover and refrigerate overnight. Bring back to room temperature before cooking.

7. POULTRY

Chicken and turkey take on a special flavour on the barbecue. Both are tender meats which are ideal for this method of cooking. Most of the recipes in this section are based on chicken, but there is no reason why you should not replace it with turkey breast fillets for equally delicious results.

Barbecue tips
● Chicken breasts, drumsticks and thigh portions are ideal for barbecue cooking, as are turkey breasts, fillets and escallops. I tend to avoid using whole legs and wing portions, since it is difficult to make sure the joint area is cooked, while the thinner areas easily overcook. If you do decide to cook larger pieces (half a chicken, for example) start cooking bone-side down – the bone conducts the heat and helps the poultry to cook. Alternatively, par-cook the joint in the microwave or in a conventional oven (on a low heat so that it does not brown) and finish off on the barbecue. This way, you can be confident they will be cooked

through.

● Refrigerated poultry should be allowed to come back to room temperature before barbecuing. This takes about an hour.

● Brush poultry pieces with melted butter, oil or marinade before cooking.

● The texture of poultry (particularly breast pieces) can be a little dry. Add moisture and flavour by marinating for a couple of hours before cooking. If the marinade has oil as an ingredient, it will also protect the meat (particularly skinless pieces) from drying out during grilling. See page 31 for marinades.

● If the skin is left on, cut it in several places, so that flavours can penetrate the lean meat.

● Oil the barbecue grid before adding the poultry pieces.

● Cooking times will depend on the size and shape of meat, its starting temperature, and the barbecue heat. Here is a general guide:

Chicken breasts, boned or part-boned – 20–25 minutes
Chicken drumsticks and thighs – 20–30 minutes
Large chicken joints/small half chickens – 30–45 minutes
Turkey breast fillets – 4–5 minutes on each side

● Poultry must always be well cooked throughout. To test it, insert a skewer or sharp knife into the thickest part. The juices should run clear. If they are still pink, carry on cooking.

Spanish Chicken
Serves 4

Spain is famous for its olive oil, tomatoes, onion, peppers and olives. This dish makes use of all of them.

4 chicken breasts
45ml (3 tbsp) olive oil
45ml (3 tbsp) tomato purée
1 clove garlic, crushed
½ green pepper, deseeded and chopped finely
1 small onion, chopped finely
6 green olives, stoned and chopped finely
2.5ml (½ tsp) chilli powder

1. Make two or three slashes in the skin side of the chicken breasts.

2. Mix together the remaining ingredients and coat the chicken on all sides.

3. Cover and marinate for at least two hours.

4. Cook over a medium heat, turning occasionally, for 20–25 minutes or until the juices run clear when the chicken is pierced with a skewer.

Serve with green salad, Cucumber Salad (page 138) and Garlic Bread (page 145).
● Can be prepared a day ahead. Complete steps 1–3 and refrigerate overnight. Bring back to room temperature before cooking.

Teryaki Chicken
Serves 4

An aunt gave me this recipe after a visit to a friend in New
Orleans several years ago.

125ml (4 fl oz) dark soy sauce
25g (1 oz) sugar
60ml (4 tbsp) white wine
2 spring onions, finely chopped
1 clove garlic, crushed
15g (½ oz) root ginger, peeled and finely chopped
8 chicken thighs

1. Mix together the first six ingredients, blending them
    well.

2. Coat the chicken in the marinade, cover and refriger-
    ate for 2 hours or more. Turn the chicken pieces over
    in the marinade once or twice during this time.

3. Grill over a medium heat, turning occasionally, for
    about 25 minutes, or until the juices run clear when
    the chicken is pierced with skewer.

Serve with hot noodles or rice and/or Marinated
Mushrooms (page 137).
●   Can be prepared a day ahead. Complete steps 1 and
    2, cover and refrigerate overnight. Bring back to
    room temperature before cooking.

Tandoori Chicken
Serves 6

This recipe is a 'must' if you are having a barbecue with an Indian theme. It is very simple to prepare.

6 chicken breasts, boned
150ml (5 fl oz) natural thick yoghurt
1 garlic clove, crushed
5ml (1 tsp) chilli powder
2.5ml (½ tsp) ground coriander
2.5ml (½ tsp) ground ginger
Rind and juice of half a lemon
To garnish:
Lemon wedges
Chopped coriander

1. Make a few shallow cuts in the skin side of each chicken breast.

2. Blend together the yoghurt, garlic, spices and lemon rind and juice. Coat the chicken pieces well with the spiced yoghurt. Cover and refrigerate for 2 hours or more.

3. Grill over a medium heat for about 25 minutes or until the juices run clear when the chicken is pierced with a sharp knife or skewer. Turn them occasionally during cooking.

Serve with Pillau Rice Salad (page 140) and a salad of sliced cucumber, tomato and onions.
● Can be prepared a day ahead. Complete steps 1 and 2, cover and refrigerate overnight. Bring back to room temperature before cooking.

Chicken in Coconut and Lime
Serves 4

The unlikely combination of coconut, chilli, lime and honey, makes a delicious 'coat' for the chicken.

50g (2 oz) creamed coconut, chopped
1 garlic clove, crushed
2.5ml (½ tsp) chilli powder
Grated rind and juice 1 lime
10ml (2 tsp) clear honey
Good pinch turmeric
4 chicken breasts, skinned and boned
Lime wedges for serving

1. Heat the coconut with 30ml (2 tbsp) water until it melts into a paste.

2. Blend together the garlic, chilli powder, lime rind and juice, honey and turmeric, and stir this into the coconut. Allow the mixture to cool.

3. Make several slashes in the chicken pieces. Spread the coconut and lime paste over the chicken, working it into the cut areas. Cover and refrigerate for 2 hours or more.

4. Grill over a medium heat for about 25 minutes or until the juices run clear when the chicken is pierced with a sharp knife or skewer.

5. Garnish with lime wedges.

Serve with hot rice or Simple Rice Salad (page 134).
● Can be prepared a day ahead. Complete steps 1–3, cover and refrigerate overnight. Bring back to room temperature before cooking.

Spatchcock Chicken
Serves 4

The garlic and freshly grated lemon zest add flavour to the often-bland meat of poussin.

2 poussins weighing 500–700g (1¼–1½ lb) each
2 cloves garlic, peeled
40g (1½ oz) butter
Grated rind 1 large lemon
Freshly ground black pepper
5ml (1 tsp) paprika

1. Using poultry shears or strong kitchen scissors, cut off the parson's nose. Cut through the ribs along each side of the backbone and remove it. Open up the chicken and turn it breast side up. Using the heel of your hand, press the bird flat so that the wishbone breaks. Secure the flat shape by inserting two skewers diagonally through the bird. Repeat with the other chicken.

2. Make several small incisions in the skin of the chicken. Cut the garlic into slivers and insert these in the cuts.

3. Melt the butter and blend in the remaining ingredients. Brush the mixture over the chickens. Cover and refrigerate for 2 hours or more.

4. Grill over a medium heat for about 30 minutes, turning occasionally, or until the juices run clear when the thigh is pierced with a sharp knife.

Serve with new potatoes or vegetable kebabs.
● Can be prepared a day ahead. Complete steps 1–3, cover and refrigerate. Bring back to room temperature before cooking.

Dusky Chicken with Melon
Serves 8

This mixture of hot spices is based on a traditional spice paste used in East Africa. The spices are first dry-fried to intensify their flavour. The melon is added as a refreshing garnish.

2.5ml (½ tsp) each of ground allspice, cardomom, cinnamon, coriander, ginger, mustard powder and turmeric
5ml (1 tsp) each of cayenne pepper, chilli powder, paprika, salt and ground black pepper
60ml (4 tbsp) red wine
15ml (1 tbsp) oil
15ml (1 tbsp) orange juice
4 chicken breast portions
4 wedges melon

1. Mix together all the spices and seasonings and heat, in a dry pan, stirring occasionally for about 2 minutes.

2. Add the red wine, oil and orange juice and stir over a gentle heat for a further minute. Allow to cool.

3. Rub the paste over the chicken portions, cover and refrigerate for 2 hours or more.

4. Grill over a medium heat for 20–25 minutes, turning occasionally, until the juices run clear when the chicken is pierced with a skewer.

Serve with the melon wedges and a dressed green salad.
● Can be prepared a day ahead. Complete steps 1–3, cover and refrigerate overnight. Bring back to room temperature before cooking.

Chicken 'Cordon Bleu'
Serves 8

Like traditional Chicken Cordon Bleu, the chicken is filled with ham and cheese. When you want something a little different, use smoked ham and a very firm cheese such as Greek Halloumi. You will need some wooden cocktail sticks. Soak them in water for an hour before use so they don't burn.

8 chicken breasts, boned
175–225g (6–8 oz) cheese, such as Cheddar, Gouda or
  Gruyère
8 small slices ham
45ml (3 tbsp) olive oil
15ml (1 tbsp) white wine vinegar
30ml (2 tbsp) chopped mint

1. Using a sharp knife, cut horizontally into the thickest part of the chicken breast, not quite all the way through, to make a pocket.
2. Cut the cheese into eight fingers and wrap a slice of ham around each (enclosing it completely). Push a ham and cheese parcel into each of the pockets in the chicken. Secure with wooden cocktail sticks (soaked in water for one hour first) or small metal skewers.
3. Mix together the remaining ingredients. Put the chicken breasts in a non-metallic dish and pour over the mixture. Turn the chicken in the marinade to coat it well. Cover and refrigerate for 2 hours or more.
4. Grill over a medium heat for about 25 minutes or until the chicken juices run clear when the meat is pierced with a skewer.

Serve with a salad of tomatoes and pasta (either hot and buttered, or cold – see Pasta Salad, page 141).
● Can be prepared a day ahead. Complete steps 1–3, cover and refrigerate overnight. Bring back to room temperature before cooking.

Chinese Chicken Drumsticks
Serves 6

This recipe was passed on to me by a Chinese friend of a friend! Five-spice powder is available in good supermarkets, oriental food stores and health food shops. It helps to have a food processor for this recipe.

3 cloves garlic
45ml (3 tbsp) soy sauce
45ml (3 tbsp) tomato ketchup
45ml (3 tbsp) soft brown sugar
30ml (2 tbsp) dry sherry or rice wine
15ml (1 tbsp) chopped fresh root ginger
10ml (2 tsp) five-spice powder
1 bunch spring onions, chopped roughly
Salt and pepper
12 chicken drumsticks
30ml (2 tbsp) clear honey
15ml (1 tbsp) lemon juice

1. Blend or process all the ingredients except the chicken, honey and lemon juice.
2. Pour the paste over the drumsticks, coating them well. Cover and refrigerate for at least two hours, preferably overnight.
3. Grill over a medium heat, turning frequently and brushing with any extra marinade, for 20–25 minutes or until the juices run clear when the thickest part of the drumstick is pierced with a skewer.
4. Meanwhile, heat the honey and lemon juice in a small pan on the edge of the barbecue.
5. Just before serving, brush the honey and lemon glaze over the chicken.

Serve with hot noodles or Simple Rice Salad (page 134).
● Can be prepared a day ahead. Complete steps 1 and 2, cover and refrigerate overnight. Bring back to room temperature before cooking.

Turkey and Bacon Burgers
Serves 4–8

Make these burgers thick or thin – to suit your taste and the occasion.

450g (1 lb) turkey, minced
4 rashers bacon, finely chopped
4 spring onions, chopped
40g (1½ oz) fresh breadcrumbs
1 egg, beaten
1 clove garlic, crushed (optional)
2.5ml (½ tsp) ground mace
Salt and black pepper
Oil for brushing

1. Mix all the ingredients well. Divide into four or eight portions and shape into burgers.

2. Brush with oil and grill over a medium heat for 15–25 minutes, depending on the thickness of the burgers. Turn two or three times during cooking.

Serve thick burgers with Traditional Barbecue Sauce (page 35) and plenty of green salad. Serve thin burgers with relish and slices of cucumber or gherkin in a soft bun (toasted on the barbecue if liked).
● Can be prepared a day ahead. Complete step 1, cover and refrigerate overnight. Bring back to room temperature before cooking.

Stuffed Turkey Rolls
Serves 4

These are good served in place of a traditional roast. Buy the turkey thighs ready boned. You will need some wooden cocktail sticks. Soak them in water for an hour before use so they don't burn.

175g (6 oz) good quality sausagemeat
Rind and juice of 1 lemon
30ml (2 tbsp) fresh thyme
Salt and black pepper
4 boneless, skinless turkey thighs
4 rashers rindless smoked back bacon
30ml (2 tbsp) oil

1. Mix together the sausagemeat, lemon rind, half the lemon juice, thyme and seasoning. Shape into four sausages.
2. Open out the turkey thighs, using a sharp knife. Lay a sausage down the centre of each and close them up again.
3. Stretch the bacon with the back of a knife and wrap a rasher around each turkey thigh. Secure with small skewers or wooden cocktail sticks (soaked in water for 1 hour first).
4. Whisk the remaining lemon juice with the oil and brush it over the turkey rolls. Cover and refrigerate for 1 hour or more.
5. Grill over a medium heat for about 30 minutes, or until cooked right through. Turn them occasionally and baste with the remaining marinade during cooking.

Serve with Cumberland Sauce (page 38) and barbecued vegetables.
● Can be prepared a day ahead. Complete steps 1–4, cover and refrigerate overnight. Bring back to room temperature before cooking.

8. KEBABS

What can be more appealing, either on the barbecue or on the plate, than a colourful concoction of vegetables, fish or meat, threaded onto skewers. Just look at the front cover of this book if you need persuading!

Skewering food is a useful way of using small quantities of meat or fish – maybe from the freezer. You could even combine foods and flavours on one skewer to please the tastes of individual members of your party. It is also a good way of using small amounts of the more expensive, speciality cuts. A shark steak, for instance, can easily be divided between four kebabs with vegetables.

Kebabs also save space on the barbecue if you have many mouths to feed. You will be more likely to fit several neat chicken kebabs on the barbecue grid, than the same number of chicken joints for example.

Barbecue tips
● Use flat rather than round skewers, or the food will slip as the kebabs are turned on the barbecue.

● Metal skewers are best. Wooden and bamboo skewers

tend to scorch and burn. If you do decide to use wooden kebab sticks, soak them in water for at least an hour before cooking to prevent this.

- Ideally, skewers should be long. If they have wooden handles, make sure they sit off the edge of the grid to avoid scorching.

- Oil skewers before threading on the pieces of food – they will slide off easier after cooking.

- Combine foods with similar cooking times – prawns, mushrooms and tomatoes; or chicken, onion and courgette, for example.

- Meats which are suitable for kebabs include chicken and turkey breast; beef steaks; pork fillet; fillet, shoulder or leg of lamb; bacon; liver; kidney, sausage. Cut the meat into bite-size cubes.

- Fish and shellfish which are suitable for kebabs include thick cod or salmon, huss, monkfish, sword-fish, tuna, shark, scallops and prawns. Cut the fish into bite-size chunks.

- Vegetables which are suitable for kebabs include onions, courgettes, aubergines, baby corn, cobs of corn (cut into rings), mushrooms and peppers. Use cooked new potatoes, sweet potatoes, carrots, parsnips, firm tomatoes and Jerusalem artichokes too.

- Marinate chunks of meat or fish before threading onto the skewers.

- Leave a small space between the food pieces as you thread them onto the skewers – they will cook more evenly.

- Brush the kebabs with oil, melted butter, a marinade, or a baste of soy sauce and honey (page 32) before grilling.

Spring Kebabs
Serves 4

This simple combination of new potatoes and baby onions is delicious.

16 small new potatoes, scrubbed
12 baby onions, peeled
30ml (2 tbsp) oil
30ml (2 tbsp) clear honey
30ml (2 tbsp) light soy sauce
30ml (2 tbsp) fresh chopped herbs, such as mint, tarragon, marjoram
Salt and black pepper

1. Boil or microwave the potatoes until just tender. Blanch the onions by immersing in boiling water for a minute or two, or microwave them with 15ml (1 tbsp) water for 2 minutes.

2. Thread the vegetables alternately onto four skewers.

3. Whisk together the remaining ingredients and pour over the skewered vegetables. Cover and marinate for ½–1 hour.

4. Lift the skewers out of the marinade. Grill them over a medium heat for about 5 minutes each side, until brown, basting frequently with the marinade.

Serve with salads and Mustard and Cheese Bread (page 146) or with meat, poultry or fish.
● The vegetables can be cooked the day before and refrigerated. On the day of the barbecue, continue with steps 2–4.

Smoked Sausage Sticks
Serves 4

The smoked pork sausage is already cooked, so it needs only a brief time on the barbecue. Don't be put off by the black treacle – it's delicious!

1 small onion
30ml (2 tbsp) oil
30ml (2 tbsp) black treacle
30ml (2 tbsp) wholegrain mustard
454g (16 oz) packet smoked pork sausage
1 large yellow pepper, deseeded

1. Peel and quarter the onion and chop very finely. Add the oil, treacle and mustard and mix together well.

2. Cut the sausage into 2.5cm (1 in) lengths and stir them into the marinade. Cover and refrigerate for at least one hour.

3. Cut the pepper into squares and thread them onto skewers with the sausage chunks.

4. Grill over a medium heat for 10–15 minutes, turning often, and basting with the remaining marinade.

Serve in crusty bread rolls or with Simple Rice Salad (see page 134).
● Can be prepared a day ahead. Complete steps 1 and 2, cover and refrigerate overnight. Bring back to room temperature before cooking.

Marinated Quorn Brochettes
Serves 4

The quorn (see page 119) quickly absorbs the flavours of this simple yet tasty marinade made from store-cupboard ingredients.

15ml (1 tbsp) oil
15ml (1 tbsp) lemon juice
15ml (1 tbsp) soft brown sugar
15ml (1 tbsp) wholegrain mustard
15ml (1 tbsp) Worcestershire sauce
15ml (1 tbsp) tomato purée
Pinch garlic salt
2.5ml (½ tsp) ground ginger
225g (8 oz) Quorn
1 red pepper, deseeded and cut into pieces
1 small onion, quartered and divided into layers

1. Blend the first eight ingredients well and stir in the quorn, coating it well. Cover and marinate for 15 minutes.

2. Thread the quorn onto skewers with the pepper and onion pieces. Brush with the remaining marinade.

3. Grill over a medium-high heat for 5–10 minutes until golden brown.

Serve as a starter or with Garlic Bread (page 145) and a salad of sliced tomatoes and onion rings.

Pork and Olive Kebabs
Serves 4

Here is a simple way to add a real Mediterranean flavour
to a meal.

30ml (2 tbsp) grapeseed or olive oil
Juice and rind of 1 lemon
30ml (2 tbsp) tomato purée
15ml (1 tbsp) soft brown sugar
15ml (1 tbsp) chopped parsley
Salt and freshly ground black pepper
450g (1 lb) lean pork, such as tenderloin
20 green olives stuffed with pimento

1. Mix together the first six ingredients in a non-metallic
    dish.

2. Cut the pork into cubes and stir into the marinade.
    Cover and refrigerate for 2 hours or more.

3. Thread the pork and olives alternately onto skewers.
    Grill over a medium heat, turning frequently, for
    15–20 minutes or until the pork is cooked through.

Serve as a starter or in sticks of French bread with a salad
of sliced tomatoes.
● The pork can be prepared a day ahead. Complete
  steps 1 and 2 and refrigerate overnight. Bring back to
  room temperature before cooking.

Cheese Bundles
Serves 4

The saltiness of the goats' cheese is offset by the sweetness of the chutney – an unusual combination, but it works! The vine leaves can be fresh or pre-packed (available from delicatessens and health shops).

16 vine leaves
200g packet Feta cheese
45ml (3 tbsp) mango chutney
4 firm tomatoes
Olive oil

1. Boil the vine leaves for 3 minutes, then drain and dry them.

2. Cut the cheese into 16 cubes and place one piece on each vine leaf. Top the cheese with a small amount of mango chutney. Fold the vine leaves around the cheese to make small bundles.

3. Quarter the tomatoes and thread them alternately with the cheese bundles onto four skewers.

4. Brush with oil and grill over a medium heat for about 10 minutes, turning occasionally. The vine leaves should be crisp but not burnt.

Serve as a starter or in toasted pitta bread.
● Prepare up to 4 hours ahead. Complete steps 1–3, cover and refrigerate. Bring back to room temperature before cooking.

Oriental Tofu Kebabs
Serves 4

Quick-cooking vegetables like mushrooms and cherry
tomatoes are ideal for skewering with firm tofu. Canned,
drained baby corn are delicious too.

15ml (1 tbsp) light soy sauce
15ml (1 tbsp) dark soy sauce
15ml (1 tbsp) clear honey
15ml (1 tbsp) sesame oil
15ml (1 tbsp) dry sherry or rice wine
Pinch of garlic salt
Pinch of five-spice powder
Freshly milled black pepper
250g (8 oz) plain, firm Tofu, cut into cubes
8 button mushrooms
8 cherry tomatoes

1. Blend the first eight ingredients well and pour over
    the tofu. Coat the pieces well, cover and marinate for
    30 minutes.

2. Thread the tofu on to skewers with the mushrooms
    and cherry tomatoes. Brush with the remaining
    marinade.

3. Grill over a medium heat for 5–10 minutes until
    golden brown.

Serve as a starter or with a salad of shredded Chinese
leaves and spring onions, and Cucumber Salad (page 138).

Vegetable Skewers with Lentil Dhal
Serves 6

Vegetarians and meat eaters alike will enjoy these colourful kebabs with the lightly-spiced lentil sauce.

3 fresh cobs of corn
3 medium courgettes
1 red pepper, deseeded
3 small onions
12 bay leaves (optional)

Marinade:
45ml (3 tbsp) olive oil
30ml (2 tbsp) lemon juice
30ml (2 tbsp) white wine
15ml (1 tbsp) chopped fresh herbs such as coriander, marjoram, mint or dill
2.5ml (½ tsp) salt

Lentil Dhal:
15ml (1 tbsp) oil
1 medium onion, finely chopped
1 clove garlic, crushed
175g (6 oz) split red lentils
700ml (1¼ pt) vegetable stock
10ml (2 tsp) chopped root ginger
5ml (1 tsp) ground cumin
5ml (1 tsp) ground coriander
2.5ml (½ tsp) ground turmeric
2.5ml (½ tsp) chilli powder
Salt and pepper
15ml (1 tbsp) lemon juice
25g (1 oz) creamed coconut

1. Boil the corn for 5 minutes, drain, cool and cut them into rounds 2.5cm (1 inch) thick.

2. Slice the courgettes into thick equal-sized pieces. Cut

the red pepper into squares. Cut the onions into quarters.

3. Whisk together the marinade ingredients and add the vegetables, turning them to coat them evenly. Cover and marinate for 2–4 hours, turning them once or twice.

4. Meanwhile make the dhal. Heat the oil in a large pan and cook the onion and garlic until soft and golden brown (or microwave for 3 minutes). Stir in the lentils, stock, ginger, spices and seasoning and bring to the boil. Cover and simmer for 20–25 minutes, stirring occasionally, until the lentils are soft and creamy (or microwave on medium power (50%) for a similar time). Add a little extra boiling water if the sauce becomes too thick. Before serving, add the lemon juice and coconut and stir until melted.

5. Thread the vegetables alternately onto six skewers, including two bay leaves on each (if using).

6. Grill over a medium heat for 8–10 minutes, turning them occasionally and brushing them with the marinade.

Serve with the lentil dhal.
● The dhal can be prepared a day ahead. Complete step 4, cover and refrigerate overnight.

● The dhal is suitable for freezing.

Spiced Seafood Kebabs with Citrus Sauce
Serves 4

Thin strips of streaky bacon hold the white fish in place on the kebab skewers.

75ml (5 tbsp) olive oil
Rind and juice of one small orange
Rind and juice of one small lemon
Freshly milled black pepper
2.5ml (½ tsp) ground coriander
2.5ml (½ tsp) ground cardamom
2 spring onions, finely chopped
225g (8 oz) white fish, such as cod, haddock
16 large prawns, peeled
8 rashers smoked rindless streaky bacon

1. Whisk together the first seven ingredients in a non-metallic dish.

2. Cut the fish into 16 chunks and toss them in the marinade with the prawns. Cover and allow to stand for 30 minutes.

3. Stretch the bacon rashers with the back of a knife and cut each rasher across into two. Lift the fish and prawns out of the marinade. Wrap one piece of bacon around each chunk of white fish.

4. Thread the wrapped fish onto skewers alternately with the prawns.

5. In a small pan heat the marinade and boil rapidly for a few minutes (or microwave it uncovered) to reduce it slightly.

6. Grill the kebabs over a medium heat until the bacon is crisp and the fish is cooked through – about 10 minutes.

Serve the kebabs with a little sauce dribbled over the top.
● Prepare no more than 1 hour before cooking.

Peppered Steak Kebabs with Mustard Dressing
Serves 4

Adjust the quantity of pepper in this recipe to suit your own (and your guests') preference.

Dressing:
225g carton Greek yoghurt
30ml (2 tbsp) mayonnaise
20ml (1 generous tbsp) wholegrain mustard
15ml (1 tbsp) finely chopped parsley (optional)

Kebabs:
500g (generous 1 lb) sirloin steak
Olive oil
30ml (2 tbsp) freshly-ground black pepper
1 medium onion
2 large, firm tomatoes

1. Blend the dressing ingredients, cover and allow to stand for at least 30 minutes for the flavour to develop.
2. Brush the steak lightly with olive oil and press the black pepper evenly on to all sides. Cut the steak into large cubes.
3. Peel and quarter the onion and separate the layers. Quarter the tomatoes.
4. Thread the steak, onion and tomatoes onto four skewers. Brush with olive oil and grill over a medium heat, turning occasionally until the steak is cooked to your liking.
5. Serve with the mustard dressing.

Delicious served simply with a crisp green salad and crusty bread.
● Stages 1 and 2 can be prepared a day ahead. Bring the steak back to room temperature before cooking. Assemble the kebabs up to one hour before cooking.

Chicken Satay
Serves 4

In this Malaysian dish marinated chicken is threaded onto skewers and served with a creamy peanut sauce.

4 boneless, skinless chicken breasts

Marinade:
45ml (3 tbsp) dark soy sauce
1–2 cloves garlic, crushed
15ml (1 tbsp) tomato purée
15ml (1 tbsp) oil
5ml (1 tsp) ground turmeric
2.5ml (½ tsp) five-spice powder
2.5ml (½ tsp) ground cumin
2.5ml (½ tsp) ground coriander

Sauce:
1 small onion, very finely chopped
15ml (1 tbsp) oil
100g (4 oz) smooth peanut butter
100g (4 oz) creamed coconut, diced
30ml (2 tbsp) lemon juice
30ml (2 tbsp) soy sauce
5ml (1 tsp) sugar

1. Place the chicken breasts (one at a time) between two sheets of clear film or damp greaseproof paper and beat them with a rolling pin, until approximately 6mm (¼ in) thick. Cut each piece, lengthways, into four strips.

2. Whisk together the marinade ingredients. Place the chicken in a non-metallic dish and pour the marinade over it. Cover and refrigerate for 2 hours or more.

3. Make the sauce. In a small pan, cook the onion gently

in the oil until soft but not brown. Add the remaining ingredients and heat through. Stir in 150–300ml (¼–½ pt) water, thinning it to the consistency you prefer. Keep warm.

4. Using eight skewers, thread two strips of chicken onto each, concertina style. Grill over a medium heat for 10–15 minutes or until cooked through.

5. Serve the skewers with a spoonful or two of sauce.

Serve with cucumber wedges, spring onions and rice.
- Can be prepared a day ahead. Complete steps 1 and 2, cover and refrigerate overnight. Bring back to room temperature before cooking.

Moroccan Lamb Kebabs with Minted Yoghurt
Serves 4

This recipe, and the two which follow, are very similar –
but they are all worth including.

500g (1¼ lb) finely minced or ground lamb
1 large onion, finely chopped
5ml (1 tsp) ground cumin
5ml (1 tsp) cinnamon
10ml (2 tsp) paprika
Good pinch cayenne pepper
45ml (3 tbsp) fresh coriander or parsley, chopped
Salt
150ml (¼ pt) natural yoghurt
45ml (3 tbsp) chopped mint

1. Mix the first seven ingredients together, seasoning to
    taste with salt.

2. Divide the lamb mixture into four and shape each
    portion into a long sausage around a skewer.

3. Blend the yoghurt and mint in a small serving bowl.

4. Grill the kebabs over a medium heat for about 10
    minutes, turning frequently.

Serve the kebabs with the minted yoghurt and a green
salad in crusty bread or pitta bread.

● Can be prepared a day ahead. Complete step 1, cover
   and refrigerate. Bring back to room temperature
   before cooking.

● Can be frozen. Complete step 1. Thaw thoroughly
   before cooking.

Spicy Beef Kebabs with Cucumber Raita
Serves 4

These kebabs have a dry texture which is complemented by the moistness and the 'cool' flavour of the yoghurt and cucumber dip. You need a food processor for this recipe.

½ cucumber
Salt
300ml (½ pt) natural yoghurt
1 spring onion, chopped finely
5ml (1 tsp) fresh coriander or parsley, chopped very finely
Black pepper
450g (1 lb) lean minced beef
1 medium onion, quartered
5ml (1 tsp) dried mixed herbs
15ml (1 tbsp) chopped parsley
15ml (1 tbsp) curry paste
2.5ml (½ tsp) chilli powder
45ml (3 tbsp) mango chutney, plus extra for serving

1. To make the raita, peel and deseed the cucumber and chop it finely. Sprinkle with salt and leave for one hour. Drain and dry it well. Mix together the yoghurt, onion, cucumber and coriander or parsley. Season with black pepper. Allow the dip to stand for ½–1 hour to allow the flavours to develop.

2. Place the beef, onion, herbs, parsley, curry paste, chilli powder, salt and black pepper into a food processor and process to a smooth thick paste.

3. Divide the mixture into eight and shape each piece into a long thin sausage on a skewer. (Put two on each long skewer or use eight small ones.)

4. Brush the beef with mango chutney (heat the chutney to soften it if necessary).

5. Grill the kebabs over a medium heat for about 10
    minutes or until cooked through.

These are best eaten straight off the skewer, dipped into
the cucumber raita. Offer extra mango chutney if wished.
●   Can be prepared a day ahead. Complete steps 1 and
    2, cover and refrigerate overnight. Bring back to
    room temperature before cooking.

Quick Kofta Kebabs
Serves 4

Don't be prepared to pass this recipe by – it is the simplest of the three. If you decide to try it, I think you will be as surprised and delighted as my friends and family. You need a food processor for this recipe.

450g (1 lb) lean lamb or a mixture of lamb and beef
1 medium onion, quartered
20ml (1 generous tbsp) ready-prepared concentrated mint in vinegar
Salt and black pepper
Oil

1. Place all the ingredients except the oil in a food processor and process till smooth.

2. Divide the mixture into eight or 16 and shape into thin sausages along skewers.

3. Brush with oil and grill over a high heat for about 5–10 minutes.

Serve with yoghurt flavoured with mint and sprinkled with paprika.
●   Can be prepared a day ahead. Complete steps 1 and 2, cover and refrigerate overnight. Bring back to room temperature before cooking.

9. VEGETABLES AND VEGETARIAN DISHES

Barbecues are synonymous with summertime and fresh produce. Many of the summer vegetables are suitable for grilling on the barbecue – sweetcorn, peppers, courgettes, aubergines and so on. They can be grilled to perfection – a little charred on the outside and tender inside while retaining a crispness, and the flavour is wonderful.

Whether you are a vegetarian, a would-be vegetarian, or you just enjoy vegetables and vegetable dishes, the recipes and ideas in this section are for you. I hope you enjoy them. (See also Salads, page 128; Vegetable Skewers with Lentil Dahl, page 104; Spring Kebabs, page 98; and Cheese Bundles, page 102.)

Barbecue tips
● There are two basic methods for cooking vegetables on the barbecue – grilling them just as they are, whole, halved or sliced; or wrapped in foil for cooking among the coals. If you decide to wrap them in foil,

allow your guests to open their own parcels to appreciate the delicious aroma.

● Oil the barbecue grid and kebab skewers or hinged wire grid, if using.

● Delight your guests with a platter of barbecued vegetables – thick slices of courgette and aubergine, onion wedges (white or red, secured with small skewers) and strips of peppers – brushed with oil and grilled over medium-hot coals.

Aubergines:
● Grill them whole, turning frequently, over a medium heat until the skin is black and the flesh inside is soft and creamy – about 20–30 minutes depending on their size and on the heat of the barbecue. To serve, halve them lengthways and dribble the cut surfaces with a little olive oil. Season with salt and freshly-milled black pepper.

● Slice the aubergines thickly, brush with oil (olive oil is best) and grill over a medium heat until golden brown and crispy on the edges and soft inside – about 10 minutes.

● Alternatively, skewer chunks of aubergine and brush with oil before grilling over a medium heat.

Carrots:
● Cook small, whole, unpeeled carrots until just tender – in a pan of boiling water or in the microwave. They should still be slightly crisp. Drain and cool them quickly in cold water. Dry them and cut into bite-size pieces. Thread on skewers (try adding them to the Spring Kebabs on page 98) and brush with oil before grilling over a medium-high heat until golden brown.

Corn on the cob:
● Soak the cobs of corn in water for 30 minutes. Peel back the husks but do not remove them. Pull away

and discard the silky hairs. Rinse and dry the corn. Brush the corn with melted butter or oil and pull the husks back into place over the cobs. Grill over a medium heat, turning occasionally, for 15–30 minutes until tender. Strip off the husks before serving.

● Strip the corn of husks and boil (do not add salt to the water) for 10–15 minutes. Drain, cool and dry them. *Either*, wrap in a double thickness of buttered foil and cook on the grid or in the coals for about 15 minutes, turning occasionally.
Or, brush the cobs with melted butter or oil and grill over a medium heat until golden brown, turning occasionally.
Alternatively, cut the cooked cobs into 2.5cm (1 inch) rings and thread them onto skewers for grilling. This way, they are easy to pick up with the fingers.

● Baby corn should be cooked lightly in a pan of boiling water or in the microwave, then skewered and brushed with melted butter or oil before grilling. Canned baby corn is already cooked, so use it as it is.

Courgettes:
● Trim whole courgettes and brush with melted butter or oil. Grill over a medium heat, turning frequently, for 5–10 minutes depending on their size.

● Halve courgettes lengthways or skewer thick slices, brush with melted butter or oil and grill over a medium heat for about 3 minutes each side.

● Alternatively, wrap courgettes, whole or sliced, in a double thickness of buttered foil and cook in the coals, turning frequently, for about 10 minutes.

Jerusalem artichokes:
● Simmer scrubbed, unpeeled artichokes with a dash of lemon juice for 10–15 minutes until tender. Drain and dry them. Thread the artichokes onto skewers, brush with the vegetable marinade on page 30, and grill over

a medium heat until golden brown – about 5–10 minutes.

● Alternatively, wrap cooked artichokes in a double thickness of buttered foil and cook in the coals, turning frequently for about 10 minutes.

Mushrooms:
● Large whole flat mushrooms should be brushed with oil or melted butter (try garlic butter, page 147) and grilled over a medium heat for about 2 minutes each side, until soft.

● Small whole mushrooms are best skewered and brushed with oil or melted butter before grilling for 3–5 minutes.

● Alternatively, wrap mushrooms in a double thickness of buttered foil and cook in the coals for about 5 minutes.

Onions:
● Use small or medium-size onions. Leave them in their skins, wrap them in foil and cook them in the barbecue coals. Check them after 15–20 minutes. The skins will protect the outer onion layers from burning. To serve, simply peel the skin off the onion and top with a knob of butter and a seasoning of salt and black pepper. You can shorten the cooking time by part cooking them first – in the microwave or in a pan of boiling water.

● Peel and part-cook small, whole onions. Thread them onto skewers, brush with melted butter or oil and grill over a medium heat for about 5 minutes until golden brown.

● Large onions should be cut into quarters and divided into pieces about 3 layers thick. Thread them on skewers (as they are, or with other vegetables, meat or poultry), brush with oil or melted butter and grill over a medium heat until brown – about 15 minutes.

Parsnips:
- Cook chunks of peeled parsnip in a pan of boiling water or in the microwave until just tender. They should still be slightly crisp. Drain and cool them quickly in cold water. Thread on skewers (on their own or with other vegetables) and brush with oil before grilling over a medium-high heat until golden brown.

Peppers:
- Choose green, red or yellow peppers. Brush with oil and grill them, whole, over a medium heat until the skins begin to blister and the peppers are soft – about 15–20 minutes. Turn them frequently. To serve, cut away the stalk end and all the seeds, then slice into strips or rings.

- Alternatively deseed and cut peppers into thick slices. Brush with melted butter or oil and grill over a medium heat until the skins are charred and the flesh is soft – about 5–10 minutes.

- Halve the peppers and deseed them. Fill the halves with a cooked filling. Place on a square of buttered, double-thickness foil and seal well. Cook over a medium heat or in the coals for 20–25 minutes until hot through. Turn them once or twice during cooking.

Potatoes in their jackets (topping suggestions on pages 35, 40, 131, 132, 147):
- Scrub and prick whole potatoes. Cook them in the conventional oven or in the microwave until tender.
  Either Brush the cooked potatoes with oil or melted butter and grill over a medium-high heat until the skins are crisp and brown.
  Or Wrap them in foil and grill on the rack or in the coals until the skins are crisp and brown.

Potatoes – new:
- Cook scrubbed, unpeeled new potatoes in boiling water or in the microwave until tender. Thread onto skewers and brush with oil or melted butter before

grilling over a medium-high heat until golden brown.

Potato skins:
- Scrub and prick whole potatoes and cook them in the oven or in the microwave until tender. Allow to cool. Cut the potatoes in half and scoop out their centres, leaving about 6mm (¼ in) thickness of potato on the skins. Cut them into wide strips and brush both sides with oil or melted butter. Season with salt and freshly-milled black pepper if liked. Arrange the skins in an oiled, hinged wire grid and grill over a medium-high heat until crisp and brown.

Sweet Potatoes:
- Peel and cut into chunks. Cook in boiling water or in the microwave until just tender. Thread on skewers (on their own or with other cooked vegetables or with raw mushrooms), brush with oil or melted butter and grill over a medium-high heat until golden brown.

Tomatoes:
- Skewer whole or halved tomatoes, or tomato wedges, brush with oil or melted butter and grill over a medium-high heat until brown and slightly soft. Take care – if they soften too much they will collapse and fall off the skewers.

MEAT ALTERNATIVES

Quorn*
Quorn is an excellent alternative to meat and is particularly appealing to those of us who enjoy the taste and texture of meat. This comparatively new food is vegetable in origin and is harvested from a tiny relative of the mushroom. It is low in fat and is a good source of protein and fibre.

Quorn is already cooked so it needs little preparation – very convenient for barbecue cooking. It has a mild flavour and a texture which is similar to tender lean meat.

Use it plain, brushed with oil or melted butter, and grilled over a medium heat for about 3 minutes; or marinate it first. Quorn readily absorbs flavours from a marinade in just half the time meat takes to absorb the same flavours – 30 minutes to one hour is ample. In addition, you will probably need to cut down on the normal quantity of strong-flavoured ingredients such as garlic, wine and herbs.

Quorn is available in packs from the chilled cabinets of major supermarkets. It is suitable for freezing for up to three months. Thaw overnight in the refrigerator.

Quorn can be used in place of meat in many of the recipes in this book. I have included a recipe for Marinated Quorn Brochettes on page 100 but I urge you to experiment yourself. Use any of the marinades on pages 30/31, in particular, Traditional Barbecue Sauce Marinade, page 35. Or try Quorn in the following recipes, marinating for ½–1 hour only and cooking the quorn on skewers:

● Spanish Chicken, page 86 – replace the chicken with quorn.
● Basque Fish Steaks, page 52 – replace the fish.
● Thai Beef Steaks, page 58 – replace the beef.

(*Quorn is a registered trademark of Marlow Foods Ltd.)

Tofu
This bean curd is made from a pressed purée of soya beans and has been widely used in oriental cookery for many years. It is low in fat, is a good source of protein, and is suitable for use in both savoury and sweet dishes.

The taste of tofu is bland. There are three basic types – firm, soft and silken. The firm version has a firm cheese-like consistency and lends itself to skewering on kebabs. Both firm and soft tofu can be used, mashed, in burger-type recipes, while the silken version is suitable for dips and dressings. Firm tofu is also available in smoked form and adds a distinctive flavour to a dish.

Because of its bland flavour, unsmoked tofu benefits

from marinating. It readily absorbs flavours like, wine, onion, garlic, lemon, herbs, etc. Use any of the marinades on pages 30/31. To help stimulate your own recipe ideas, I have included one for Tofu Kebabs on page 103.

Textured Vegetable Protein (TVP)
Textured vegetable protein (or TVP in short) is another vegetable product usually made from soya beans. Low in fat and rich in protein, it is obtainable in its dried form from health food shops.

TVP is usually available in natural flavour or in meat flavours, and is sold in various shapes and sizes. Follow the pack instructions for rehydrating in hot water or a well-flavoured vegetable stock.

The mince and granule versions are ideal for burger-type recipes for the barbecue, often mixed with nuts or lentils to give a 'meaty' consistency. Use it to replace minced meat in a recipe. Look out, too, for the wide range of ready-prepared 'sausages' and 'burgers' made with TVP.

Mushrooms in Garlic Cheese Sauce
Serves 6

Allow your guests to open their own foil parcels, to appreciate the wonderful aroma.

6 large flat mushrooms
142g pack cream cheese with garlic and herbs
30ml (2 tbsp) lemon juice
Salt and black pepper

1. Wipe the mushrooms. Remove and chop the stalks.

2. Cream together the cheese and lemon juice with the chopped mushroom stalks. Season to taste.

3. Divide the mixture into six and place one portion into the cup side of each mushroom. Place each mushroom on an oiled square of double-thickness foil. Seal each parcel securely.

4. Cook in the coals for about 10 minutes, turning frequently (and gently – taking care not to tear the foil).

Serve as a starter or as an accompaniment to barbecued meat, poultry or fish.
● Can be prepared a day ahead. Complete steps 1–3 and refrigerate.

Sweetcorn Packets
Serves 4

A pretty way of serving sweetcorn. When doubling up on this recipe, use one green and one red pepper for extra colour contrast.

4 cobs of corn
15g (½ oz) butter
4 spring onions, chopped
1 clove garlic, crushed
1 small red pepper, deseeded and chopped
5ml (1 tsp) paprika
Salt and black pepper

1. Strip the husks from the corn and trim if necessary. Cook them in plenty of boiling water for 10–15 minutes. Drain and dry.

2. Melt the butter in a pan and soften the onions, garlic and pepper for a few minutes (or microwave for 3 minutes). Stir in the paprika and seasoning.

3. Place each cob on a square of double-thickness foil. Pour one quarter of the sauce over each cob. Seal the parcels securely.

4. Cook in the coals for about 15 minutes, turning frequently.

Serve as a starter or as a vegetable accompaniment.
● Can be prepared a day head. Complete steps 1–3, cool and refrigerate. Bring to room temperature before cooking.

Cheese and Onion Grills
Makes 4 large or 8 small

These are particularly tasty when served with a well-flavoured sauce such as tomato.

175g (6 oz) fresh breadcrumbs, preferably wholemeal
175g (6 oz) mature Cheddar cheese, grated
4 spring onions, chopped
15ml (1 tbsp) chopped fresh sage or 5ml (1 tsp) dried
15ml (1 tbsp) mustard powder
2 eggs, size 3
Salt and pepper
Sesame seeds
Oil for brushing

1. Mix together the breadcrumbs, cheese, spring onions, sage and mustard powder. Stir in one whole egg and one egg yolk to bind the mixture.

2. Divide into four and shape each portion into four large, or eight small, cakes. Cover and refrigerate for 2 hours or more.

3. Lightly beat the remaining egg white and brush it over the cheese and onion cakes. Dip them in sesame seeds (use as few or as many as you like).

4. Brush the cakes with oil and grill over a low-to-medium heat until golden brown and the cheese is melting throughout.

Serve with Tomato Sauce (page 37) or Traditional Barbecue Sauce (page 35) and a crispy green salad.
● Can be prepared a day ahead. Complete steps 1–3, cover and refrigerate overnight. Bring back to room temperature before cooking.

Peppers with Cracked Wheat Filling   *Serves 6*

You will love the fresh flavours and colours in this simple-to-prepare recipe.

300ml (½ pt) vegetable stock
100g (4 oz) bulgar wheat
1 onion, sliced finely
15ml (1 tbsp) oil
2 large tomatoes, skinned and chopped
30ml (2 tbsp) chopped parsley
30ml (2 tbsp) chopped mint
Salt and black pepper
3 yellow or red peppers, or a mixture
25g (1 oz) toasted flaked almonds, to garnish

1. Bring the vegetable stock to the boil and stir in the bulgar wheat. Remove from heat and allow it to stand for 10 minutes to absorb all the stock.
2. In a small pan, soften the onion in the oil until golden brown (or microwave for 3 minutes). Stir in the tomatoes and cook for a further minute. Add the herbs. Stir the mixture into the bulgar wheat and season to taste with salt and black pepper.
3. Halve the peppers lengthways and scoop out the seeds. Divide the stuffing and fill the pepper halves.
4. Place each pepper half on a square of double-thickness, buttered foil. Fold the edges to secure them well.
5. Grill over a medium heat for 20–25 minutes, turning the packets a few times. The peppers and the stuffing surface should be golden brown. Garnish with toasted almonds to serve.

Alternatives: omit the mint and add some dried fruit (sultanas or chopped, ready-to-eat apricots); replace bulgar wheat with couscous or cooked rice.

Serve as a starter or as a main course with mixed salad and garlic bread.

● The stuffing can be prepared a day ahead. Complete steps 1 and 2 and refrigerate.

Grilled Stuffed Aubergines
Serves 4

These savoury stuffed aubergines can be a meal in themselves. As an accompaniment, they go well with vegetable kebabs, sausages or chicken.

2 medium aubergines
60ml (4 tbsp) olive oil
1 medium onion, chopped
1 large clove garlic, crushed
227g can tomatoes, drained
15ml (1 tbsp) chopped fresh oregano, or 5ml (1 tsp) dried
30ml (2 tbsp) chopped parsley
100g (4 oz) cooked brown rice
175g (6 oz) mature cheddar cheese, grated
25g (1 oz) toasted pinenuts
Salt and freshly milled black pepper
Grated Parmesan cheese or toasted breadcrumbs to garnish

1. Halve the aubergines lengthways. Use a small spoon to scoop out the centres, taking care not to split the skins. Chop the aubergine flesh into small pieces.
2. Heat the oil in a pan and cook the onion and garlic with the aubergine pieces until soft and golden brown. Stir in the remaining ingredients (except the Parmesan or breadcrumbs).
3. Pile the mixture into the aubergine shells.
4. Place each aubergine half on a square of double-thickness, buttered foil. Fold in the edges and secure well.
5. Grill over a medium heat for 20–30 minutes, depending on the size of the aubergines.

Serve each guest their own parcel and allow them to sprinkle over grated Parmesan or toasted breadcrumbs, if using.

● Can be prepared a day ahead. Complete steps 1–4 and refrigerate overnight. Bring back to room temperature before cooking.

Spicy Lentil Cakes   *Serves 8*

These tasty cakes can be prepared well in advance. They are baked in the conventional oven first.

30ml (2 tbsp) oil
1 large onion, finely chopped
1 large garlic clove, crushed
10ml (2 tsp) ground turmeric
2.5ml (½ tsp) ground coriander
2.5ml (½ tsp) ground cumin
2.5ml (½ tsp) cayenne pepper
225g (8 oz) lentils
900ml (1½ pt) vegetable stock
2 eggs, beaten
75g (3 oz) mature Cheddar cheese, grated
30ml (2 tbsp) plain flour
Salt and pepper
Oil for brushing

1. Heat the oil and cook the onion until soft and golden brown (or microwave for 5 minutes).
2. Stir in the garlic, turmeric, coriander, cumin and cayenne pepper and cook for a minute or two, stirring.
3. Add the lentils with the vegetable stock and bring to the boil. Reduce the heat and simmer gently until the lentils are soft and the mixture is very thick – 20–30 minutes. Allow to cool slightly.
4. Mix in the beaten eggs, cheese, flour and seasoning.
5. Spread the mixture into an approximate 25cm (10 in) square on an oiled baking sheet. Bake at 190°C/375°F/gas mark 5 for 20 minutes or until firm.
6. Allow to cool before cutting into 16 squares. Lift them off the baking sheet with a fish slice.
7. Brush the cakes with oil and grill over a medium heat until crisp and brown.

Serve with chutney and natural yoghurt or Tomato Sauce, page 37.
- Can be prepared a day ahead. Complete steps 1–6, cover and refrigerate overnight.
- Suitable for freezing after step 6.

10. SALADS AND SALAD DRESSINGS

No barbecue is complete without a selection of fresh and colourful salads. A simple green salad, tossed in a dressing just before serving, is hard to beat. I leave it to you to concoct your own favourite salads, but I do urge you to keep them simple. Choose two or three ingredients only – a bowl containing two types of green lettuce mixed with one red type; or sliced tomatoes and onion rings overlapping on a large platter are so much more impressive than a large bowl of mixed salad. A salad dressing is a must – a simple salad is transformed into something special with the addition of a dressing.

This section concentrates on salad dressings and composite salads which can be prepared well in advance of the barbecue, leaving you to give your undivided attention to on-the-spot cooking.

Basic French Dressing
Makes a little more than 150ml (¹/₄ pt)

Olive oil is now a popular choice for salad dressings. Try combining oils such as olive, walnut or hazelnut with lighter ones such as sunflower, soya or grapeseed.

135ml (9 tbsp) olive oil
45ml (3 tbsp) white or red wine vinegar, cider vinegar or lemon juice
10ml (2 tsp) French mustard
10ml (2 tsp) sugar
Salt and freshly milled black pepper

1.   Mix all the ingredients and whisk in a bowl or shake well in a screw-topped jar.

2.   Whisk or shake again before serving.

Use cold to dress leafy, fruit or vegetable salads; or use hot to dress hot vegetable salads (potato, pasta and rice in particular).
Store in a screw-topped jar in the refrigerator for up to 3–4 weeks. Dressings containing nut oils, cheese or cream should be stored in the refrigerator for a few days only.

Try the following variations, adding the ingredients to one quantity of the Basic French Dressing.

Mustard and Chive Dressing
Use to dress hot potatoes.
Add 30ml (2 tbsp) wholegrain mustard, 30ml (2 tbsp) chopped chives and 15ml (1 tbsp) clear honey.

Garlic and Parsley Dressing
Use to dress green, mushroom or mixed salads.
Add 1–2 crushed garlic cloves and 15ml (1 tbsp) chopped parsley.

Mint Dressing

Use to dress potatoes or salads which include fresh fruits.
Add 15ml (1 tbsp) finely chopped mint.

Blue Cheese Dressing

Use to dress salads which are to be served with steaks,
chops, or burgers.
Add 50g (2 oz) crumbled Roquefort or Danish Blue
cheese and 30ml (2 tbsp) single cream. Blend or process
until smooth.

Five-Minute Mayonnaise
Makes about 300ml (½ pt)

Use your blender or food processor to make your own mayonnaise for dips or to serve with vegetables, fish, meat and salads. Make sure the ingredients are at room temperature before use. Try adding a little olive, hazel-nut, walnut or grapeseed oil to a basic salad oil like sunflower or soya.

2 egg yolks
5ml (1 tsp) Dijon mustard
30ml (2 tbsp) white wine vinegar or lemon juice
2.5–5ml (½–1 tsp) salt
Freshly milled black pepper
300ml (½ pt) salad oil

1. Put the egg yolks, mustard and 15ml (1 tbsp) vinegar or lemon juice into the blender or food processor. Add the salt and some black pepper. Blend or process for 10 seconds.

2. With the blender/processor still running, pour in the oil gradually (in a thin trickle) until the mixture thickens.

3. Blend in the remaining vinegar or lemon juice, plus 15ml (1 tbsp) boiling water.

Store in a screw-topped jar in the refrigerator for up to one week.

Flavour home-made mayonnaise to suit the food being served (see below). Alternatively, buy a good-quality mayonnaise and add your own flavourings. For lighter dressings, combine an equal quantity of mayonnaise and natural yoghurt, sour cream, fromage frais or quark – especially good for topping potatoes in their jackets. Try the following variations, adding the ingredients to 300ml (½ pt).

Herb
Serve with fish or vegetables, particularly potatoes.
Add 60ml (4 tbsp) chopped chives, 30ml (2 tbsp) chopped parsley and 30ml (2 tbsp) single cream or natural yoghurt.

Garlic
Serve with chicken or burgers.
Add two crushed cloves garlic and 60ml (4 tbsp) single cream or natural yoghurt.

Lemon
Serve with fish or vegetable kebabs.
Use lemon juice in place of white vinegar if you make your own mayonnaise. Add the grated rind of two lemons.

Piquant
Serve with sausages, burgers or jacket potatoes.
Add 15ml (1 tbsp) chopped gherkins and 15ml (1 tbsp) tomato ketchup.

Summer Potato Salad
Serves 6–8

These baby potatoes are tossed in an oil and vinegar dressing while they are still warm. Leave their skins on. Try this recipe using the Mustard and Chive Dressing on page 129 too.

900g (2 lb) small new potatoes, scrubbed
1 quantity Basic French Dressing – page 129
Salt and freshly milled black pepper
1 bunch spring onions, chopped
Lettuce leaves for serving

1. Boil the potatoes for about 15 minutes (or microwave on full power for about 10 minutes, stirring once or twice) or until tender.

2. Drain the potatoes well, cut them in half and tip into a large bowl.

3. Season the dressing with salt and pepper to taste, stir in the spring onions and pour it over the hot potatoes. Toss together lightly. Cover and allow to stand for at least one hour, stirring occasionally.

Serve at room temperature on a bed of lettuce leaves.
● Can be prepared several hours in advance. Arrange the salad on a bed of lettuce leaves just before serving.

Simple Rice Salad
Serves 8

Make up your own colourful medley of ingredients to stir into the cooked rice.

225g (8 oz) long-grain rice
1 quantity Basic French Dressing, page 129

Three or more of the following ingredients:
1 medium red pepper, deseeded and chopped
1 medium green pepper, deseeded and chopped
1 bunch spring onions, chopped
½ cucumber, deseeded and diced
2–3 stalks celery, chopped – or 1 small bulb fennel, sliced
75g (3 oz) cooked peas
50–75g (2–3 oz) seedless raisins
227g can pineapple chunks, drained
198g can sweetcorn, drained

1. Cook the rice according to pack instructions, drain well and tip into a large bowl.

2. Add the dressing and your chosen, prepared ingredients and toss well. Cover and allow to stand for at least one hour.

Serve at room temperature.
● Can be prepared a day ahead. Cover and refrigerate overnight. Bring back to room temperature before serving.

Quick Coleslaw
Serves 8

Another recipe passed on by a friend, this fresh, crisp salad develops a beautiful 'warm' colour overnight.

1 small white cabbage, cored and sliced very finely
2 large carrots, grated
1 medium onion, chopped very finely
1 red apple, cored and chopped finely (leave the skin on)
½ quantity Basic French Dressing, page 129
60ml (4 tbsp) mayonnaise

1.   Mix together the cabbage, carrots, onion and apple.

2.   Add the French Dressing and toss gently.

3.   Stir in the mayonnaise and refrigerate overnight.

Serve at room temperature with jacket potatoes, poultry, meat or fish.
●   Must be prepared a day ahead – see method.

Grilled Pepper Salad
Serves 4–6

You and your guests will love the mellow 'Mediterranean' flavour of this colourful salad. Loosen the skins of the peppers on the barbecue or under the grill.

5 peppers – red, yellow, green or a mixture
45ml (3 tbsp) grapeseed oil or olive oil
15ml (1 tbsp) red wine vinegar
2.5ml (½ tsp) French mustard
10ml (2 tsp) clear honey

1. Grill the peppers over a medium heat on the barbecue (or under the conventional grill) until the skins blacken and loosen. Wrap them in a tea towel for 10 minutes then remove the skins.

2. Halve and deseed the peppers then cut into strips.

3. Whisk the remaining ingredients and pour over the peppers. Cover and allow to marinate for at least an hour.

Serve at room temperature with vegetables, fish, poultry or meat.

● Can be prepared up to a day ahead. Complete steps 1–3, cover and refrigerate. Bring back to room temperature before serving.

Marinated Mushrooms
Serves 4–6

A simple recipe in which button mushrooms are marinated overnight. Choose small, even-sized mushrooms.

225g (8 oz) button mushrooms
1 stalk celery, finely sliced
2 spring onions, chopped
15ml (1 tbsp) chopped parsley
30ml (2 tbsp) oil
15ml (1 tbsp) red wine vinegar
1 clove garlic, crushed (optional)
5ml (1 tsp) soft brown sugar
Salt and freshly-milled black pepper

1. Mix together the mushrooms, celery, onions and parsley.

2. Whisk together the remaining ingredients and pour over the mushrooms. Toss the salad carefully – taking care not to break the mushrooms. Cover and refrigerate for at least two hours.

Serve at room temperature with meat, poultry or fish.
● Can be prepared a day ahead. Cover and refrigerate overnight. Bring back to room temperature before serving.

Cucumber Salad
Serves 4–6

This is a refreshing salad which improves on standing.

2 medium cucumbers
10ml (2 tsp) salt
30ml (2 tbsp) white wine vinegar
30ml (2 tbsp) hazelnut or walnut oil
15ml (1 tbsp) light soy sauce
5ml (1 tsp) caster sugar
2.5ml (½ tsp) paprika
Chopped coriander or parsley

1. Peel the cucumbers and halve them lengthways.
    Scoop out the seeds and discard them. Slice the
    cucumbers, sprinkle the salt over them and refrigerate
    for ½–1 hour. Rinse well and pat dry.

2. Whisk together the wine vinegar, nut oil, soy sauce
    and sugar. Pour the dressing over the cucumber and
    toss to coat it well. Cover and refrigerate for several
    hours.

3. Just before serving, sprinkle over the paprika and
    scatter some chopped coriander or parsley on top.

Serve at room temperature with grilled fish or chicken.
● Can be prepared a day ahead. Complete steps 1 and
    2, cover and refrigerate overnight. Bring back to
    room temperature before serving.

Ratatouille Salad
Serves 4

Ratatouille originates from the French region of Provence.
It is usually served hot but is just as good when eaten cold.

45ml (3 tbsp) olive oil
1 large onion, sliced thickly
1–2 cloves garlic, crushed
225g (8 oz) courgettes, sliced thickly
225g (8 oz) aubergines, cubed
1 red pepper, deseeded and sliced thickly
1 yellow or green pepper, deseeded and sliced thickly
398g (14 oz) can chopped tomatoes with herbs
15ml (1 tbsp) tomato purée
Salt and black pepper

1. Heat the oil in a large pan and cook the onion and garlic gently until soft and slightly brown.

2. Stir in the courgettes, aubergines, and peppers and continue cooking for a couple of minutes. Add the tomatoes, tomato purée and 60ml (4 tbsp) water. Season well.

3. Bring to the boil then simmer gently for about 25 minutes, stirring occasionally. Allow to cool.

Serve at room temperature with poultry, fish or meat.
● Can be prepared up to three days ahead. Cover and refrigerate. Bring back to room temperature before serving.

Pillau Rice Salad
Serves 6

This is a salad version of the rice dish which usually accompanies curries.

60ml (4 tbsp) oil
1 large onion, chopped
10ml (2 tsp) sugar
4 cardamom pods
2 × 2.5cm (1 inch) sticks cinnamon
4 cloves
2.5ml (½ tsp) turmeric
4 bay leaves
375g (12 oz) basmati rice
Salt

1. Heat 30ml (2 tbsp) oil and cook the onion with the sugar until soft and golden brown.

2. Add the spices and bay leaves and cook for a minute or two.

3. Stir in the rice and cook for one minute. Add 850ml (1½ pt) boiling water and salt to taste. Bring to the boil, stir once, cover and simmer gently until the rice is tender and the liquid has been absorbed (about 15 minutes).

4. Tip the rice into a large bowl and stir in the remaining 30ml (2 tbsp) oil. Allow the rice to cool then separate the grains with a fork.

Serve at room temperature with vegetables, meat or fish.
● Can be prepared up to a day ahead. Cover and refrigerate overnight. Bring back to room temperature before serving.

Pasta Salad
Serves 6

Pasta salads so often include a mayonnaise dressing. Try this tomato, lemon and pesto dressing for a change. Buy pesto sauce from good supermarkets.

225g (8 oz) pasta shapes, such as spirals
1 small lemon
30ml (2 tbsp) olive oil
1 red or white onion, sliced thinly
1 clove garlic, crushed
230g can chopped tomatoes
30ml (2 tbsp) pesto
10ml (2 tsp) sugar
Salt and freshly ground black pepper

1. Cook the pasta according to pack instructions and drain.

2. Pare the rind off the lemon, using a potato peeler. Cut into strips. Squeeze out the juice.

3. Heat the oil in a pan and cook the onion and garlic until soft and golden brown (or microwave for 3 minutes).

4. Stir in the tomatoes, pesto, sugar, lemon rind and juice and seasoning. Bring to the boil and simmer for a few minutes (in the microwave, if you wish).

5. Pour the sauce over the warm pasta and stir gently. Cover and allow to cool, stirring gently occasionally.

Serve at room temperature with vegetables, poultry or fish.
Variation: stir in a can of drained red kidney beans at stage 5.
● Can be prepared a day ahead. Cover and refrigerate overnight. Bring back to room temperature before serving.

Mediterranean Vegetable Salad
Serves 6–8

Raw vegetables are marinated to make a lovely crunchy salad. The colour combination is spectacular.

225g (8 oz) broccoli, cut into small florets
1 small or ½ large cucumber, peeled and sliced thickly
1 red onion, sliced
1 green pepper, deseeded and sliced
1 red pepper, deseeded and sliced
2 carrots, sliced
100g (4 oz) black olives
100ml (7 tbsp) olive oil
45ml (3 tbsp) lemon juice
15ml (1 tbsp) soft brown sugar
2.5ml (½ tsp) mixed dried herbs
1 clove garlic, crushed
225g (8 oz) cherry tomatoes
Salt and black pepper
15ml (1 tbsp) parsley, chopped
45–60ml (3–4 tbsp) grated Parmesan cheese (optional)

1. Combine the first seven ingredients in a large, non-metallic bowl.

2. Whisk the olive oil with the lemon juice, sugar, herbs and garlic. Pour the dressing over the vegetables and toss to coat them evenly. Cover and refrigerate for several hours, preferably overnight, stirring once or twice.

3. Stir in the tomatoes, seasoning and parsley. Serve sprinkled with Parmesan cheese if liked.

Serve at room temperature with poultry, meat or fish.
● Can be prepared a day ahead – see method. Bring back to room temperature before serving.

11.   BREADS AND BUTTERS

Do take every opportunity to warm up bread sticks and bread rolls on the barbecue – to produce the 'freshly baked' aroma and flavour that we all appreciate. It only takes a minute or two and is well worth the effort.

Although it is possible to make breads such as pizza, chappatis and naan on the barbecue, there are perfectly acceptable products available in good supermarkets today. These are just as nice, warmed through on the barbecue to achieve the smoky flavour. Alternatively, make and bake your own recipe conventionally – ready to heat through on the barbecue.

Here are some ideas for toasted sandwiches and for flavouring breads to be heated in the oven or on the barbecue.

Quick barbecue-toasted sandwiches

These are superb for feeding hordes of hungry children or teenagers at a party. Prepare stacks of them in advance.

Prepare one or more of the following fillings and use them to fill slices of white or wholemeal bread (buttered on the outside), pitta bread, split Focaccia (flat Italian bread). For a change, use one of the savoury butters on page 147 in place of plain butter. Toast on the barbecue over a medium-heat until golden brown and crispy on the outside and the filling is warmed through. Turn the 'sandwiches' with a fish slice or with tongs, or use an oiled, hinged wire grid if you think they are in danger of falling apart.

Filling suggestions:
Ham slices and cheese
Cheese and grated apple mixed with lemon juice
Grated cheese and pickle
Grated cheese, tomato slices and finely chopped onion
Smoked ham slices with chopped celery in mayonnaise
Cooked chicken pieces with Lemon Mayonnaise (page 132)
Flaked smoked mackerel, lemon juice, black pepper, and
    a little horseradish sauce
Cream cheese with dates and walnuts
Cold, cooked hamburger with Piquant Mayonnaise
    (page 132) or pickle
Danish Blue cheese and seedless black grapes
Sliced cold cooked sausages with piccalilli or apple sauce

Garlic Toast

Use thick slices of fresh bread, or cut a French stick diagonally into 2.5cm (1 in) slices. Spread both sides of the bread thinly with garlic butter (page 147). Grill over a medium-high heat until crisp and brown.

Alternatively, rub a cut garlic clove over diagonal slices of French bread then brush with oil (olive oil is delicious). Grill over a medium-high heat until crisp and brown.

Garlic Bread

Soften one quantity of garlic butter (page 147). Make diagonal cuts into a French stick nearly, but not quite, all the way through. Spread the garlic butter in the slits and push the loaf back into shape. Wrap in a double thickness of foil. You may find it easier to halve the loaf and make two parcels in order to fit the whole stick on the barbecue. Grill over a high heat, or in the coals, for about 10 minutes, turning frequently.

Mustard and Cheese Bread
Serves 6–8

This is a good starter to any barbecue meal, whetting the appetite for the good things to follow! Hand out paper napkins to wipe buttery fingers.

100g (4 oz) butter
15–30ml (1–2 tbsp) Dijon mustard
100g (4 oz) Gruyère or Gouda cheese, grated
1 French stick

1. Soften the butter and blend in the mustard and cheese.

2. Make diagonal cuts into the bread nearly, but not quite, all the way through. Spread the butter into the cuts. Wrap the loaf in a double thickness of foil. You may need to cut it in half and make two parcels in order to fit the whole stick on the barbecue.

3. Grill over a high heat, or in the coals for about 10 minutes, turning frequently.

Serve as a starter or with vegetable kebabs.
● Can be prepared several hours or a day ahead. Complete steps 1 and 2, wrap and refrigerate until needed.

Savoury Butters

Use savoury butters to:
   top plain barbecued vegetables, fish or meat,
   accompany fresh crusty rolls,
   flavour bread as in garlic bread (page 145) or garlic toast
      (page 145)
   add a melting garnish to hot vegetables, rice or pasta,
   cook vegetables or fish in foil parcels on the barbecue.

Garlic Butter
Soften 100g (4 oz) butter and blend in two or three
crushed garlic cloves. Season with a little salt and freshly
milled black pepper if liked. Spoon into serving dishes.
For butter which will slice – spoon the mixture onto a
square of foil, roll up like a sausage, twist the ends like a
Christmas cracker and chill until firm. To use, unwrap the
butter and cut into slices with a sharp knife which has been
dipped in hot water.

ALTERNATIVES:
Follow the method given for garlic butter, replacing the
garlic with one of the following ingredients.

Parsley Butter
Add 30ml (2 tbsp) chopped parsley and a good squeeze of
lemon juice.

Herb Butter
Add 60ml (4 tbsp) chopped fresh herbs of your choice –
such as chives, tarragon, dill, thyme, parsley, basil. Use
only small quantities of strong herbs such as sage or
rosemary.

Lemon Butter
Work in 30ml (2 tbsp) fresh lemon juice and the grated
rind of one small lemon.

Mustard Butter
Stir in 30ml (2 tbsp) French or wholegrain mustard.

Blue Cheese Butter
Crumble in 75g (3 oz) Roquefort or Danish Blue cheese and blend till smooth.

Tomato Butter
Chop 4 or 5 sun-dried tomatoes (drain off the oil) and blend into the butter till smooth.

Sweet Butters

Use sweet butters spread on brioche or bread slices for toasting on the barbecue; brushed over fruit kebabs; or to top fresh fruit for cooking in foil parcels on the barbecue (page 152).

Sweet Lemon Butter
Soften 100g (4 oz) unsalted butter. Work in 30ml (2 tbsp) lemon juice, the grated rind of one small lemon and 15ml (1 tbsp) or more icing sugar or clear honey. The amount of sweetener used will depend on what the butter is to be used for, and on your personal preference. For butter which will slice, use the method given for garlic butter, on page 147.

ALTERNATIVES
Follow the method given for lemon butter, replacing the lemon juice and rind with one of the following ingredients:

Orange Butter
Work in 30ml (2 tbsp) orange juice and the grated rind of one orange.

Cinnamon or Ginger Butter
Add 5ml (1 tsp) ground cinnamon or ginger and sweeten to taste.

Coconut Butter
Work in 30–45ml (2–3 tbsp) desiccated coconut (plain or toasted) and sweeten to taste.

Nut Butter
Work in 50g (2 oz) chopped walnuts, pecan nuts or toasted hazelnuts and sweeten to taste.

Rum or Brandy Butter
Add 15–30ml (1–2 tbsp) rum or brandy and sweeten to taste.

12. SWEET THINGS ON THE BARBECUE

When you are eating out of doors, maybe away from home, or you are entertaining a crowd, it makes sense to prepare as many parts of the feast as you can in readiness for the barbecue. Then you can relax in the knowledge that 'everything is organised' and enjoy the time with your family and guests. I have resisted the temptation to fill this section with make-in-advance desserts. There are plenty of good cookery books with recipes for mousses, sylla-bubs, cheesecakes, trifles, flans, gateaux, and so on. In any event, your guests will always appreciate a colourful bowl of fresh fruit salad, topped with cream, yoghurt or ice cream.

   In the next few pages, then, I have concentrated on giving ideas and recipes for my favourite sweet things *on the barbecue* – to take advantage of the heat left in the coals. Use these suggestions when you have the time to prepare them, and on the occasions when the number in your party is not too large.

Barbecue tips
- Cooking times will depend on the heat of the coals at the end of a barbecue. Move the grid close to them – you will be surprised how much heat is left. If you have a gas barbecue, there is no problem.

Apples:
- Bake them in double-thickness buttered foil. Use *small* eating apples, core them and make a cut around the centre of each. Fill with marzipan or a mixture of brown sugar, cinnamon and sultanas; or honey and chopped ready-to-eat apricots. Wrap securely in the buttered foil and grill on the barbecue rack for about 40 minutes, turning two or three times during cooking.
- Cut cored eating apples into segments and thread onto skewers. Brush them with melted butter and sprinkle with mixed spice if liked. Grill over a medium heat for about 5 minutes or until golden brown. Turn them over half way through cooking.

Bananas:
- Grill whole bananas on the barbecue grid until their skins blacken – about 5 minutes each side, depending on the heat of the coals. To serve, make a slit in the skin along the length of the banana and pour in a little honey or maple syrup. Use a teaspoon to lift out the hot, sweet banana.
- Peel bananas, brush them with melted butter and wrap securely in a double thickness of buttered foil. Grill on the barbecue rack or in the coals until the banana is soft – about 5 minutes. Serve with yoghurt mixed with a little honey, with cream or with ice cream.

Bread and cake:
- Cubes of brioche and firm cake, such as Madeira, are delicious skewered with fresh fruits, brushed with melted butter and grilled until golden brown.

● Toast sweet pikelets or waffles on the barbecue and top with ice cream and raspberry coulis (page 157).
● Make hot cinnamon toast to serve with fresh fruit salad or ice cream – thinly butter both sides of a slice of bread, sprinkle with sugar and cinnamon and grill over a medium-high heat until golden brown on both sides.

Cheese:
● Grill firm cheese such as goats' cheese and Halloumi (brushed with oil first) to serve with fresh fruit.

Marshmallows:
● Toast them individually on the end of a skewer or kebab stick. Be quick or they will melt all over the coals!

Mixed fruit:
● Fruit kebabs look delightful and taste wonderful. Skewer chunks of fresh fruit (choose from apricots, peaches, nectarines, plums, greengages, pineapple, figs, stoned cherries, mango, papaya, large strawberries, eating apples and orange segments). Brush the kebabs with melted butter and sprinkle over a little icing sugar for those with a sweet tooth. A sprinkling of ground cinnamon, ginger or mixed spice is a warming addition on a chilly evening. Grill until golden.
● Make fruit parcels by cutting fruits into small pieces and wrapping one portion securely in a double thickness of buttered foil. Add a little fruit juice, sherry, brandy or liqueur if liked. Grill on the barbecue grid until the fruit is hot and beginning to soften – about 5 minutes. This method is particularly suitable for raspberries and blackberries.

Black Bananas with Butterscotch Sauce
Serves 4

These bananas are delicious served just as they are, with whipped cream, or with this simple sauce. The bananas will sit on the barbecue quite happily while the main course is eaten.

Sauce:
50g (2 oz) butter
75g (3 oz) light soft brown sugar
90ml (3 fl oz) maple syrup
150ml (¼ pt) double cream
Few drops vanilla essence

4 bananas

1. Make the sauce in a small saucepan or in the microwave. Heat the butter, sugar and maple syrup slowly until the butter has melted. Stir in the double cream and vanilla essence. Keep warm (on the side of the barbecue if there is room).

2. Grill the bananas over a medium heat until black on the underside – about 5 minutes. Turn them over and repeat with the second side.

Serve the bananas with the skins split lengthways and the butterscotch sauce dribbled inside.
● The sauce can be prepared in advance and heated just before serving.

Normandy Kebabs
Serves 4

Use crispy red and green apple wedges, threaded alternately onto kebab sticks and see how attractive they look
– both on the barbecue and on the plate.

4 apples
Juice of 1 lemon
50g (2 oz) unsalted butter
50g (2 oz) caster sugar
45ml (3 tbsp) Calvados or brandy

1. Core the apples and cut each one into eight wedges.
   Cut each wedge in half crossways. Toss the pieces in
   lemon juice to prevent them discolouring.

2. Melt the butter and stir in the caster sugar. Continue
   heating gently until the sugar dissolves. Add the
   Calvados or brandy.

3. Thread the apple onto eight small skewers and brush
   with the sweetened butter.

4. Grill over a medium heat for about 5 minutes, turning
   once. Brush the kebabs with the butter several times
   during cooking.

Serve any excess butter dribbled over the hot kebabs.

Baked Bananas with Brandy Sauce
Serves 4

Another simple way of serving bananas off the barbecue –
with a creamy sauce.

Small carton Greek yoghurt
25g (1 oz) icing sugar
45ml (3 tbsp) brandy
4 bananas
Juice of 1 lemon
45ml (3 tbsp) toasted, chopped nuts

1. Whisk together the Greek yoghurt, icing sugar and
    15ml (1 tbsp) brandy. Chill until needed.

2. Peel the bananas and slice them thickly onto four
    squares of double-thickness foil. Sprinkle with the
    remaining brandy and the lemon juice.

3. Fold up and seal the parcels securely.

4. Grill over a high heat, or in the coals, for 3–5 minutes.

Serve topped with the chilled sauce and sprinkled with
toasted nuts.
● The sauce can be prepared up to a day ahead.
    Complete step 1, cover and chill until needed.

Pineapple with Stem Ginger
Serves 4

Allow each guest to open their own pineapple parcel – the aroma is lovely.

4 slices fresh pineapple, about 2cm (¾ in) thick
2 pieces stem ginger in syrup
2.5–5ml (½–1 tsp) ground cinnamon
20ml (4 tsp) port (optional)

1. Skin and core the pineapple slices. Lay each one on a large, double sheet of buttered foil.

2. Halve the pieces of stem ginger and place one half in the centre of each pineapple slice. Dust with cinnamon and sprinkle over some extra ginger syrup. Add 5ml (1 tsp) port to each, if using.

3. Fold up and seal the parcels securely.

4. Grill over a medium heat for 5–8 minutes, turning occasionally.

Serve with chilled whipped cream.
● Can be prepared up to 4 hours ahead. Complete steps 1–3 and refrigerate.

Fruit Cups with Raspberry Coulis
Serves 6

Use really ripe pears, peaches, nectarines or even apricots. A blackberry coulis is delicious too – replace the raspberries with the same quantity of blackberries. It helps to have a food processor for this recipe.

350g (12 oz) fresh raspberries, thawed if frozen
30ml (2 tbsp) sweet white wine (or use water)
30ml (2 tbsp) icing sugar
3 soft ripe pears
200g packet low-fat cream cheese
15ml (1 tbsp) caster sugar
Few drops vanilla essence
30ml (2 tbsp) chopped toasted nuts

1. Blend or process the raspberries with the wine or water, and the icing sugar.

2. Peel, halve and core the pears. Place each half on a square of double-thickness foil.

3. Blend together the cheese, caster sugar and vanilla essence. Pile a spoonful of the cheese into each pear half and sprinkle the nuts over. Close the foil parcels, sealing the edges securely.

4. Grill the pears in their parcels, right way up, over a medium heat for about 10 minutes.

Serve with a pool of raspberry coulis.

● Step 1 can be prepared a day ahead.

● The raspberry coulis is suitable for freezing.

INDEX

If you would like an up-to-date list of all RIGHT WAY titles
currently available, send a stamped self-addressed envelope to
**ELLIOT RIGHT WAY BOOKS, LOWER KINGSWOOD,
TADWORTH, SURREY, KT20 6TD**
or visit our web site at www.right-way.co.uk